STEP
BY
STEP

JUDY SCHAFER

STEP
BY
STEP

A FAMILY'S JOURNEY
TO THE SUMMIT
OF MOUNT RAINIER

1TW
PRESS

Published by 1TW Press, Edgewood, WA
1twpress.com

Edited and designed by Girl Friday Productions
www.girlfridayproductions.com

Cover design: Rachel Marek
Project management: Sara Addicott
Editorial: Tiffany Taing
Illustration credit: bootprint © OpenClipart-Vectors/Pixabay

Cover photos from the author's personal collection.

ISBN (paperback): 978-1-7365105-0-6
ISBN (ebook): 978-1-7365105-1-3

Library of Congress Control Number: 2021905938

Dedicated to Kris and Tim,
the best climbing partners ever.

And to Ember—may you inherit
your dad's thirst for adventure.

"I would rather be ashes than dust!

I would rather that my spark should burn out in a brilliant blaze than it should be stifled by dry-rot.

I would rather be a superb meteor, every atom of me in magnificent glow, than a sleepy and permanent planet.

The function of man is to live, not to exist.

I shall not waste my days trying to prolong them.

I shall use my time."

—Jack London

CONTENTS

ONE TOUGH WOMAN

A rock dislodged under my foot and rolled a few inches down the loose, sandy soil of the steep hillside. I stopped and looked up to estimate how much longer it would take to get around the large rock outcropping that loomed above me. Once I made my way past it, the route would turn to climb straight up the slope through jagged rocks, loose sand, and pumice toward my goal: St. Elmo Pass at the head of Glacier Basin in Mount Rainier National Park.

Voices drifted to my ears on the still, cool air, and I heard phrases like ". . . really big pack . . ." and ". . . headed straight up. . . ." As I stopped to catch my breath, I searched the glacial rubble below until I spotted the source. Two men stood on the main trail below me, where it wound between boulders, gravel, and small patches of green near the bottom of Inter Glacier. Their upturned faces gazed in my direction.

"Are you going up?" The shouted question reached me on the soft breeze as the taller man gestured at St. Elmo Pass.

I turned and looked up the slope. I realized I hadn't quite made it halfway up the steep incline after leaving the main trail. I still had about three hundred feet of altitude to conquer before reaching the low spot on the rocky ridge above me. It could easily take another twenty minutes of climbing.

I faced the men and took a deep breath. "Yeah!"

I could see the smile on one man's face as he hollered back, fist raised, thumb pointed to the sky. "You're one tough woman!"

Uncertain how to respond, I waved back with a smile. The men couldn't know that the oversize daypack on my back carried little more than my lunch and extra clothing. Aside from food and water, most of the contents added little weight. I didn't consider myself tough. More like driven. Driven to spend time in the outdoors and to experience adventures, sometimes sharing those things with my boys. And driven to push myself to my limits.

As the murmur of the men's voices faded into the distance, I turned back to the challenge of picking my way up the loose, rocky slope below the pass. Another stone dislodged and rolled several feet downhill, making dull, hollow *clunks* as it hit other volcanic rocks.

Am I really tough, I thought, *or just a little reckless?*

Several steps later, I emerged from the shadow of the outcrop and headed directly up the remaining incline. Almost immediately, I spotted fresh footprints in the sandy patches scattered between the loose, volcanic rocks and gravel. Pausing again to catch my breath, I examined them. I searched the slope above and soon spotted a figure moving purposefully through the rocks toward the ridgeline. I had hoped I might have the place to myself, but I was disappointed.

The previous day, an article in the paper had announced that after this first weekend in October 1999, the Park Service would be closing the road to this part of Mount Rainier National Park for the winter. Weather reports had predicted clear skies on Saturday, and I'd been unable to resist the chance for one last hike to Glacier Basin. Now the sun shone with deceptive warmth, and the clear blue sky made it hard to believe the end of the hiking season in the Park had arrived.

Other hikers had also decided to take advantage of the great weather and visit this part of the Park one last time before the winter snow flew. On the way up, I'd shared the trail with several other groups of hikers. Campers' tents filled the sites at the Glacier Basin campground as I passed through. Once I'd climbed higher, I even spotted a tent perched on a ridge above the basin just below Mount Ruth.

Most of today's hikers had stopped at the end of the maintained trail in Glacier Basin or a half mile above, near an old mine site. Few day hikers continued the extra half mile to the base of Inter Glacier, and fewer still tackled the side trip up to St. Elmo Pass. To get there, a hiker had to leave the main trail that led to Inter Glacier and on up to Camp Schurman. The pass perched 500 feet above the terminus of the glacier, almost 1,500 feet higher in elevation than Glacier Basin. It was a dead end, but it offered a great view of the Winthrop Glacier on the other side of the ridge. I should have known, though, that on a Saturday with weather as agreeable as this, I would run into at least one other adventurous hiker.

As I tackled the last few feet of the ascent, I saw that the hiker, a gray-haired man in a wool T-shirt and gray hiking pants, now sat on one of the rocks at the crest. I wondered if he planned to stick around, or if he would head down soon. I took the final few steps to flat ground and found a big flat rock to set my pack on.

Turning his attention from the view, he smiled at me. "Hi," he said. A long-sleeved shirt was tied around his waist.

"Hi," I answered as I dug into my pack. A slight breeze blew over the ridge from the Winthrop Glacier, just enough to chill the sweat on my back.

"Beautiful weather, isn't it?" he said.

"Sure is. Pretty unusual for this time of year." I peeled off my outer shirt and replaced it with a warmer dry one.

"Are you from around here?" he asked.

"Yeah, I live near Tacoma. How about you?" I sat on the rock and pulled a first aid kit out of the bottom of my pack.

He explained that he was Canadian, though staying briefly in Yakima. He said he had hiked extensively in the Canadian Rockies with his daughter. She had summited Mount Rainier recently with friends, and she wanted to do it again, with him. He'd heard that this trail was one of the routes up Rainier, and he wanted to check it out.

"Yeah," I commented. "The route most people climb is on the other side, through Camp Muir, but this is the second most-used route. It seems to be getting more popular all the time."

He watched as I peeled off my boots and socks and then started applying moleskin and adhesive tape to my heels.

"It would be a great accomplishment," I said, "to climb it with your daughter. I climbed Rainier with my two sons last year."

His eyes widened. "You've been to the summit?"

"Actually, I've been to the top several times." I stopped and calculated. "Somewhere around six or seven. But the most rewarding time was with my boys last year. They were"—I paused to think—"twenty and seventeen at the time." I rounded up the age of Kris, my firstborn.

"Do you really need ropes and crampons for the climb?"

"You don't dare try it without them," I told him. "On these glaciers, all it takes is one fall into a crevasse without a rope and you're dead."

"Do people climb it in one day?"

"Only if they live here, and then usually only on a dare. Most people hike up to Camp Schurman or Camp Muir, stay the night, and then head the rest of the way up early the second day."

"How early?" he asked.

"On a hot day in summer they might start around midnight or one o'clock. That's so the snowbridges over the crevasses will still be firm when they're descending. A lot of people continue down the afternoon of their summit attempt, but on this route, I like to come down to camp again, spend a night resting up, and then hike out the next day."

We discussed tactics and necessary skills for a few more minutes. Then he stood up and grabbed his day pack. As he slung it on his back, he said, "Sorry to have intruded on your solitude."

"No problem. I hope I didn't ruin yours."

"Not at all. I appreciate the information." He headed down the rudimentary trail toward the valley floor below.

I finished my bandage job and put my boots back on.

After he left, I realized that in many ways, I was glad for the chance to share this beautiful day, this amazing scenery, and my experiences with someone. I nestled down between two rocks, out of the breeze, to enjoy the view and the last sunshine of the season.

Looking back on that hike in 2000, I realize that one statement I made to the hiker revealed what I believe to be one of the most cherished achievements in my life: that I had reached the summit of Mount Rainier with my boys.

Not long ago, I headed to Mount Rainier for yet another hike with Tim—my younger son, who had recently turned thirty-eight. While we walked, he told me about a conversation he'd had at work after returning from a mountain biking trip.

"I've noticed all the outdoor activities you enjoy, like cycling, skiing, and mountain climbing," my son's coworker told him. "You must be really glad that you had a dad who would take you out and teach you all those things."

Tim laughed. "It wasn't my dad. It was my mom!"

I had to laugh with him when he told me the story. My trips with Tim and Kris are some of the most treasured times of my life. I wouldn't give them up for anything. And I love sharing them with other people.

Hikes, climbs, bike rides, canyons, and mountains provide the background for many memories of our adventures together. As I've told stories about them to my friends, they've encouraged me to share them with a wider audience. In this book, I focus on narratives, originally written as stand-alone stories, leading up to and including our journey to the top of Mount Rainier. I hope you enjoy them.

THE JOURNEY
BEGINS

The last step depends on the first.

—René Daumal

Backpacking gear and a borrowed pack lay strewn across our living room floor and couch. I stepped away from my organizing and looked around, feeling a sudden unease.

What in the world am I doing? I thought. *Should I really be planning to take my son, who won't be seven until next week, backpacking by myself?* Sure, I was bringing Tesha along. I figured our 110-pound malamute would be able to both carry some gear and intimidate anyone who might consider bothering us. *Still,* I wondered, *is this going to work?*

I shoved the doubts aside and dove back into arranging gear. My goal was to keep my pack as light as possible. When I'd hiked the Rocky Mountains before getting married, I'd been able to keep my pack under 30 pounds. The Cascades were different. Campfires were discouraged, so a stove and fuel had to be added to the gear. And Kris wouldn't be carrying much of anything.

I was only five foot three, but I had kept myself in shape by playing tennis and walking. I'd always felt that God had given me extra strength for my size. I still got carded at the ballpark when I ordered beer. One look at my youthful face, and the server would ask for my ID. At thirty-five, I still felt young and had gained enough experience to know that if I didn't overload my pack, I would be able to handle it.

Kris wandered into the living room. I took in my little guy. "Are you ready for this?"

His short sandy-brown hair was lighter than my own long brunette tresses. The bangs across his forehead framed a smiling face. His solid build could have been designed with backpacking in mind. Tall for seven, he'd lost his baby fat. Yet he weighed more than most of his friends of the same height—a sign of his sturdiness.

His sapphire eyes, brighter than my blue-green irises, surveyed the mess. "Yeah, Mom. I'm ready. When are we leaving?" He really had no idea what he was or was not ready for.

"Do you think you can carry this?" I held up his little blue school pack, which I'd stuffed with a lightweight down sleeping bag.

He worked his arms into the straps, then walked with a jaunty step into the kitchen and back. "Yeah, Mom," he said. "I can do that."

I sure hope so, I thought. *I hope you can keep it up for four miles.*

I had been busy for the first ten years of my marriage settling into married life, having kids, and raising them out of toddlerhood.

As the boys grew, I realized how much I missed backpacking. The difference between driving to a campground or day hiking versus hiking in for an overnight stay loomed large in my mind. An overnight trip I'd taken with our local malamute club to Pete Lake near Cle Elum had proven that our dog, Tesha, could handle a pack. That trip was the sum total of my post-marriage backpacking experience. Larry, my husband, just wasn't interested in carrying a pack out on a trail to camp in the woods.

By August 1986, I was ready to get back outdoors to do some of the things I had always loved. I craved time in the outdoors. I decided to take Kris backpacking.

Once my pack was full, I weighed it. It was close to my 30-pound goal. Tesha's pack carried our tent and her dog food. It weighed in around 15 pounds—nowhere near the amount she was capable of carrying. And Kris's small pack, with his sleeping bag and a few snacks, didn't weigh much more than 4 pounds.

I'd chosen our destination because I had experience hiking the trail. Years before, I'd participated in a young adult group at Glendale Lutheran Church near Seattle. One of our activities had been a backpacking trip to a small lake in the North Cascades near Mount Shuksan called Lake Ann. The trail started not far past the Silver Fir campground, about two miles before a viewpoint of Mount Baker named Artist Point.

The lake was four miles from the trailhead, and I remembered it being an easy trek. We had taken the pastor's two small children with us, who were about three and five at the time. The older child, a boy, even carried a very small pack. I pushed aside the memory of the times when some of the big, strong guys in our group had carried the kids on their shoulders for short distances during the hike. After all, I had a dog who was built to carry weight, and I figured she would be a big help with our gear.

God blessed Kris and me with beautiful weather as we headed north to Bellingham and then east into the mountains where we found the trailhead. Butterflies in my stomach did their best to discourage me as we put on our packs and headed to the trail. But I picked up Tesha's leash, looked at Kris with his little pack, and said, "Okay, let's go!"

Then I looked down at the path winding through tall Douglas firs toward a valley below. *Oh, darn!* I thought. *It'll be uphill on the way back.*

We hiked for a mile and a half, then came upon a small creek flowing through a green, flower-strewn meadow at the bottom of the valley. We stopped for a lunch break and sat on rocks near the creek.

"How are you doing?" I asked Kris as he munched on peanuts and chocolate chips from our bag of trail mix. Hikers at this time usually called it gorp.

"I'm fine," he said. "How much farther is it?"

"Not too far. Pretty soon we'll be halfway there."

Though I'd let her off leash for most of the hike, Tesha had shown little inclination to run off. Now she wandered toward the creek. "I better stop her before she rolls in the water with her pack," I told Kris.

I let Tesha take a drink, led her back to our rest spot, and adjusted her pack. It tended to sag on the side where I had tied the tent, despite my attempts to keep the load balanced.

We greeted other hikers as they passed by our rest spot. I noticed a couple of them eyeing us with amusement. I wasn't bothered, because so far everything was going according to plan and my unease was dissipating.

After about twenty minutes, I said, "Time to get moving."

We took off through the green grass and wildflowers of the valley floor. The trail soon began to climb through thick forest, growing steeper and steeper as it led to a small saddle, a low spot in the ridge above us. We would need to cross over that before reaching the lake. We lost the protection of the forest as the trees grew smaller and farther apart. The last section of trail below the saddle switchbacked through rocky talus slopes, and we trudged under the hot sun. The unfamiliar exertion challenged both of us. I tried to set a slow pace for Kris, but I still found myself out of breath.

"Can we stop?" I heard Kris's young voice from behind me.

"Sure," I said. A great excuse for a break.

We repeated this pattern three or four times on the last uphill push. Several small groups passed us coming down the trail from the lake.

"Not much farther," an older gray-haired gent offered.

Soon, another hiker encouraged us: "You're almost there."

Finally, we reached the saddle. Together, Kris and I looked out at the panorama before us. Lake Ann lay nestled in a depression on a rocky shelf spread out below and to our right. Beyond the lake, the ground dropped away into a deep valley. On the other side of the valley rose Mount Shuksan, a dark rocky bastion festooned with hanging glaciers and permanent snow fields. The ridge we stood on continued to rise to our left, then curved around and ascended to meet the bulk of Mount Shuksan. I tried to take it all in.

Looking down at the lake, I spotted a few tents decorating the bare ground along the far lakeshore. Beyond them, a narrow line of alpine trees grew at the very edge of the steep drop-off. A couple more tents had been set up on flat ground near the south end of the lake, close to the base of the ridge.

We set off down the path toward the far side of the lake. A well-beaten trail continued on to the left along the ridge, but we turned to the right, following the shoreline to the area where we'd seen tents set up.

A bare, flat site called out to us. Kris and I shrugged off our packs and set about putting up our little yellow tent. Occasionally we heard a deep rumble from across the valley. Each time the sound caught our attention, we examined the face of Mount Shuksan. Torrents of snow fell from hanging glaciers and sifted through black rocks on the near-vertical face, reminding me of lacy waterfalls. Clouds of airborne snow crystals billowed up around them.

Once our camp had been established, I said, "Shall we explore a little?"

"Sure," Kris said enthusiastically.

Before long we found the toilet. A steep, narrow trail led downhill from the bench by the lake through small juniper bushes and twisted dwarf pines toward a wooden box, perched on the steep slope that plunged into the valley below.

This couldn't be called an outhouse. It had no walls. The box had a hinged lid and sat over a hole dug for the collection of waste. Its construction was crude, but its location provided the most spectacular view a person could ever ask for. A full view of the west face of Mount Shuksan across the valley filled us with awe.

We realized we would need to rely on the buddy system when we had to go. Someone had to stand at the top of the trail to let other people know it was occupied.

Next, Kris and I, with Tesha following closely, headed out on the trail that skirted the upper basin of the valley. Climbers use this main trail to access the Fisher Chimneys—a steep, rocky escarpment that tops out on Lake Ann Buttress, a ridge extending east from the mountain. The route makes its way up these dangerous cliffs, notorious for rockfall. Once they've conquered this challenge, climbers traverse south across a glacier to a small saddle, crossing the face of the mountain but gaining little altitude. From there, the route turns north and follows a ridge toward the steep black pyramid of the summit.

Not far along the trail, we found a small creek flowing through grass and wildflowers, tumbling down from the ridge to the valley below.

"This will be a great place to get our water," I said. "We'll have to treat it, but it will be nice and cold for drinking." I'd brought iodine pills along so I could purify any water we collected.

Once back in camp, I thought about how to cook our ramen and sausage for dinner. At one point when I looked for Kris, I saw him talking to a couple of men who had set up their tent in the adjacent site.

I headed toward their camp. "Is Kris bothering you?"

"No, not at all." I took in a slightly built, dark-haired man, with a little gray showing at his temples. He continued. "We're having a great chat." He seemed to be in his early forties.

"They're going to climb Mount Shuksan!" Kris's voice was filled with excitement and awe.

The man introduced himself as Rick. "I work at the Seattle REI store, Recreational Equipment, Incorporated. It's a co-op that sells outdoor gear."

"I've been there a few times," I said. "There's so much cool camping gear there. And I love their greeting cards with all those wildflowers and scenery. That's usually all I can afford."

Rick turned to his younger companion. "This is Steve," he said. Steve stood taller, with a stockier build. Sandy-brown hair framed his friendly face.

"I work at REI, too, in their carpentry shop," Steve told us. "We build the wooden displays that the stores use."

I introduced myself and asked, "When do you start climbing?"

"We're going to spend the first part of the night here at Lake Ann and then get up real early to head up the Chimneys," Rick said. "We want to climb before the glaciers soften up." He looked sheepish as he then asked, "Do you happen to have any extra food? I walked out of my house this morning and left all of my breakfast and lunch food on my kitchen counter."

"Nobody ever does anything like that," Steve ribbed him.

It felt good to be able to help out these friendly outdoors-men. I thought about what I had packed and made an offer. "We have plenty of gorp, and I have beef jerky, too."

"Um. I'm a vegetarian, so I think I'll pass on the jerky. But I'll take you up on the gorp, if it's okay with you. I'll even let you use my binoculars tomorrow while we climb, in trade." He made his appreciation clear.

I went to our tent and found my bag of mixed munchies, then took it back and traded with Rick for his binoculars.

Kris and I wished them good luck as we headed back to our camp.

When bedtime came, I wasn't sure what I should do with Tesha. With two people already sleeping in our small tent, it didn't have room for a big dog, too. I was happy when she curled up just outside our tent door. She stayed in place the whole night.

Kris and I planned to spend two nights at Lake Ann, so we spent the day in between exploring. We followed the climbers' trail to the base of the Chimneys, then hiked back and climbed the ridge behind the lake, where we had a great view of the mountain. Using Rick's binoculars to follow climbers as they made their way up and down Mount Shuksan through ice, snow, and rocks proved to be great fun. On a completely different route to the right of the summit, we spotted a string of climbers making their way across a snowy slope far below the summit ridge. We kept tabs on them as they wandered back and forth across the steep, south-facing glacier.

"Do you think they're lost?" Kris asked.

"They might be." They never did ascend to a place where they could approach the top of the mountain, and eventually they disappeared in the rocks near the bottom of the valley.

Rick and Steve arrived back at their camp not long after lunch. Kris listened with rapt attention as they told us about their climb.

"Thanks for the food," Rick said again. "It was a lifesaver."

While we watched them pack up their gear before heading out, Kris announced, "I'm going to climb Mount Shuksan just like them someday." That was the first time I'd ever heard him express an interest in mountain climbing. The seed had been planted.

"Okay," I said. The two climbers looked on with amusement. "That's an interesting goal." Kris and I watched as the guys shouldered their heavy climbing packs and took off down the trail.

After another restful night, Kris and I began our own hike toward home under a hot sun set in azure skies that continued to drive away any clouds. Just as I'd imagined, we conquered the trail down from the lake easily. Then we crossed the valley and started up through the forest toward the trailhead. It was hard not to complain about the uphill trek. But it wasn't long before we reached our car and shrugged off our packs.

"That was great," I said to Kris with enthusiasm. "Did you like it?"

"Yeah, it was fun," he said with a grin.

"So, you'll go with me again?"

"Sure. And I really do want to climb Mount Shuksan someday."

I knew our trip had been a success.

The end of summer was rapidly approaching, so there wouldn't be another trip before winter. I looked forward to next year and another adventure.

Little did I know what lay ahead.

FIRST CLIMB:
A PRELUDE

They who wait for the Lord shall renew their strength;
They shall mount up with wings as eagles;
They shall run and not be weary;
They shall walk and not faint.

—Isaiah 40:31

After taking Kris on his first backpacking trip in 1986, I began to make plans for the next year, but my plans came to an abrupt halt. I tore my ACL in January, in a snow-tubing accident. Instead of getting in better shape by hitting the trails during the summer, as I'd planned, I hobbled around on crutches with a full-length cast until June. Several more weeks passed before I could limp along on a leg that could only extend 160 degrees and bend to 90 degrees—and this was with a 190-pound muscular guy pushing as hard as he could to bend and straighten my leg during physical therapy.

While faithfully going to physical therapy three times a week, I spent considerable time paging through the magazines the clinic provided to their patients. There were times during each visit when I sat with a heat pack, and then later with an ice pack, wrapped around my knee. It was during one of these treatments that I discovered *Outside* magazine, which is devoted to stories about people who spend their time hiking, climbing, and exploring the outdoors. Not all the stories focused on hard-core adventurers. I also found articles that described people just like me, average people who got outdoors and left the comfort of their couches behind.

I particularly came to enjoy an author named Tim Cahill. He wrote very descriptively and with humor about a broad range of outdoor topics. His articles covered his experiences in trying activities beyond his comfort zone, like rock climbing. I learned that he lived in Livingston, Montana, the town where I had lived during the formative years of my youth, from ages four to fourteen.

I enjoyed his stories so much that I bought one of his books, and then another. They were collections of some of the articles he had written. I was thrilled when I came upon a story in one of his anthologies that described the constant wind in Livingston. This wind, he wrote, caused a newly installed wind turbine planted on the flats above town to shimmy in a "mad polka" until it threw a blade and collapsed to the ground. As a child, I'd overheard my parents talk about how the wind could blow over a hundred miles an hour and knock over semitrucks crossing the flat bench above the river valley. My classmate and I, making our way home from kindergarten, had made up a fantastical story about a supernatural panther roaming the land—our way of explaining the phenomenon.

When I was at physical therapy, I sat in a white room on a brown padded bench with my knee wrapped in frosty towels, and my imagination escaped to a world of trees and rocks, glaciers and mountaintops.

Kris's declaration from the year before came to mind. "I'm going to climb Mount Shuksan just like them someday," he'd said about the climbers we met. This memory planted the seed for my own goal, though I picked a different mountain.

I'll climb Mount Rainier, I decided. *I'll do it next year. It'll give me something to work toward.*

The term *bucket list* wouldn't enter America's consciousness until the release of the 2007 movie of the same name, starring Jack Nicholson and Morgan Freeman. The idea of compiling a list of things to do before I died had never entered my thoughts, but I was in the habit of coming up with significant goals. I usually developed these one or two at a time in response to events in my life. I rarely looked forward more than a year. These plans gave me something exciting to look forward to and a reason for exercising, keeping in shape, and being active. The anticipation offset the effects of the gray Pacific Northwest winters that pushed me toward depression every year.

Tackling Mount Rainier was only the first of these goals that involved climbing. Other mountains in the Cascades, like Mount Baker and Glacier Peak, would eventually be added to the list. Other adventures, including hiking the Wonderland Trail and rafting rivers in the Southwest, would provide further variety. Eventually, I realized I was a risk-taker and adrenaline junkie. But all that would come later. In the summer of 1987, I was still working on walking normally again.

At first, as my physical therapist and I tried to get my knee mobile, my doctor told me, "You're just not working hard enough to loosen it up."

This was the same doctor who'd initially told me, "You don't have to get surgery. You could just be careful what you do, and wear a brace."

Are you kidding?! I'd thought. *I'm not ready for a rocking chair on a porch!* I had the surgery within a week.

In October, however, he finally suggested that I undergo a second surgery to clean the scar tissue out of my joint. In November, he completed the procedure. When he saw me in my hospital room afterward, he admitted, "There was so much scar tissue in your knee, no one could have broken it loose, no matter how hard they tried."

It's about time you believed me, I thought.

During the summer, I'd run across an old friend, Pastor Ken Smith. Tall, spare, and sandy-haired, he was just a little older than me. We had both been involved in a Bible study for couples back when he was an assistant pastor at our church. He was now leading his own congregation in Centralia, Washington.

As we caught up, I brought up my new ambition. "I've been reading all about mountain climbing," I told him. "It helps keep me motivated."

"I've climbed Mount Rainier before. Three times, actually," he said.

"Really? That's something I'd like to do. When my knee is better."

"When you're ready, maybe I could round up some people to go on a climb," he suggested.

He returned for a visit to our church on Thanksgiving weekend. I walked up to him on crutches, only a week out from surgery. "Okay," I said. "I'm ready to start planning for that Mount Rainier climb next summer."

He looked at me with what might have been skepticism, or maybe it was just amusement.

"Do you think you could still organize a group to go?" I asked him. "I really want to do it."

"Okay," he said. "I'll talk to the climbers I know. I can probably get a group of people together."

I'm sure after he saw me limping away, he didn't think about it again. After all, I was walking with crutches, my body had softened with inactivity by that point, and I carried a few extra pounds. But in my mind, it was entirely possible.

As the weeks passed and 1988 arrived, I gained strength and flexibility. My physical therapist supported my climbing goal and at first even expressed an interest in going along. Eventually, he decided not to go, but he kept up his support. I reached out to Ken several times to update him on my progress and find out how his end of the planning was going.

I continued to work hard at physical therapy. A machine I used to strengthen my legs required me to lie prone while pushing on a foot platform attached to heavy-duty black bands with varying levels of resistance. My therapist told me the machine had been developed to help astronauts maintain muscle mass in space. My quads grew stronger every week.

By April of 1988, I was ready to get out and try a real trail. I headed for Mount Si, a small mountain east of Seattle, where hikers gain 3,100 feet in just under four miles. Some people are familiar with it as one of the mountains in the TV show *Twin Peaks*.

A hiker friend of mine had told me, "Everyone who wants to climb Mount Rainier trains on that trail."

And so, I headed for the popular trail on a typical Northwest spring day, with clouds scudding overhead and patches of blue hinting at better things to come. My legs felt great as I followed the switchbacks up the hill through the forest to the bare rocks at the top. I didn't scramble up the last little rocky point, the Haystack, but enjoyed my lunch on a big rock in the sunshine during a break in the clouds.

Then it was time to go back down the hill. My legs felt fine at first, but before long I began to feel weaker. By the time I reached the parking lot, my calves felt wrecked. This was when

I realized I had done plenty of training for climbing uphill, but nothing for coming back down.

For the next couple of days, I suffered through a soreness in my calf and leg muscles worse than any I had ever felt before, or have felt since. I gingerly climbed the stairs in our church as we prepared for an Easter concert. The only way I could go down was by taking funny little hops while clinging tightly to the railing. That experience motivated me to start making circuits of the stairs in our neighborhood high school stadium several times a week while carrying a pack.

But there's more to preparing for a climb of a glaciated 14,411-foot peak than performing physical therapy exercises and climbing up and down stairs. I searched guidebooks and maps, looking for trails other than those at Mount Si that also went up and down and weren't too far from my house. Every time I could leave my six- and eight-year-old boys with someone, I slipped away from my responsibilities as a stay-at-home mom and headed for the hills. Larry supported my activities, but my mother-in-law thought my goal was reckless, and she told my husband I was being a terrible mother.

I forged ahead, the words of Jack London ringing in my head: *I would rather be ashes than dust.* I discovered this quote during a time of national mourning after the explosion of the *Challenger* space shuttle. To me, it embodied the spirit of exploration. It explained why I couldn't quit reaching for the heights.

In March, Ken told me he had lined up a few interested people. By May the number had dwindled to only two other men. One of them, John, was also a pastor in Centralia. In his fifties, with dark hair, John was five ten, a few inches shorter than Ken. The other man was one of Ken's on-again-off-again parishioners. Bob, a sixty-year-old lumber company owner, had a sturdy frame that displayed his strength. What hair he had left was gray. He had summited Mount Rainier several times and told us great stories about his experiences.

One of his anecdotes stuck with me. "Once we camped in the crater on top of Mount Rainier," he said. "It was so cold that when I made some tea and left it out while I went to relieve myself, I found it frozen solid when I came back."

He also offered great advice. "Oranges are the *best* thing to take on a climb, even though they weigh a lot. When nothing else tastes good at high elevations, they're just wonderful."

In addition to my own training hikes, Ken organized two challenging outings that I participated in. First, in May, the four of us headed to Mount Ellinor, an accessible day hike on the Olympic Peninsula near Lake Cushman. The trail isn't long, but much of it consists of steep grades that can challenge hikers. In addition to providing an opportunity for physical training, the hike gave Ken and Bob a chance to teach John and me the fine art of self-arrest—stopping yourself on a steep, icy slope with an ice axe.

At the trailhead, I shrugged into a day pack loaded with twenty-five pounds of gear, the weight Bob had suggested. "You don't need to carry more than that for training," he'd said. "Too much weight can be hard on your knees, especially when going downhill. When we actually climb, adrenaline will take over and you won't have a problem with your forty-pound climbing pack."

I fell into line behind the three men and we took off up the trail. From the car, we started up a small ridge with a steep incline. I pushed myself to keep up with my companions' long strides. Almost immediately, my legs began to burn and my breathing came in quick gasps. John struggled, too, and we stopped after about twenty minutes for a short break before continuing up.

After about forty-five minutes, my legs loosened up and my breathing settled into a fast but regular, efficient rhythm. I experienced this way of settling into a hike or climb for years, though after a while the adjustment period shortened to a half hour. Only after I had ten or fifteen years of climbing under my belt did I warm up easily at the beginning of a hike, without pain or breathlessness.

We continued up the trail in the cool morning air and then emerged from the trees at the base of a steep, snow-covered slope. John continued to struggle up the mountain, sweat pouring off his flushed face as the temperature rose.

When we stepped onto the snow, Bob and Ken explained that ascending a snowfield is very different from hiking up a bare trail. They showed John and me how the leader of a climbing party breaks trail by kicking into the snowy slope to make steps, and how the rest of the party follows in the leader's footsteps.

"It's like going up a really long staircase," Bob said.

The leader determines the length of stride and kicks steps in the snow that are usually firm and even. In this case, our six-foot leader's stride made me work hard with my short legs. Of course, breaking trail this way only applies to untouched snow. Once fifty people have been up the slope before you, all bets are off.

When we finally approached the summit, four or five white woolly mountain goats stood on top to greet us. They scampered off as we moved closer and found rocks to sit on. We ate our lunches under a sunny sky decorated by only a few scattered clouds.

While we talked, Bob pointed to a rugged, steep-sided ridge that adjoined our peak. "One time when I came up here, we reached the ridge on the other side of those cliffs. Then we had to work our way across that rock face."

"It looks dangerous," John said.

"It has a lot of exposure," Bob agreed.

This was my introduction to the term *exposure*. "It means that if you fall," Bob explained, "it's a long way down."

John turned to Ken. "I don't think I'm ready for this. I think I'll back out of the Rainier climb."

"You still have plenty of time to get in shape," Ken replied. "Keep working at it. You're going to St. Helens with us, right?" We planned to ascend Mount St. Helens as our second training hike.

John nodded.

"Wait until after that trip to decide. You'll see how much better you feel," Ken encouraged him.

Ken had folded our group into a climb of Mount St. Helens that he and some friends had already scheduled. It would take place two weeks before our Rainier trip. His permit for this climb was for a day in early June. We planned to climb Rainier near the end of the month. We'd picked midweek days both times, so we wouldn't have to fight crowds.

John's hesitation reminded me of a thought I had entertained. *Is this really something I should be spending my time on?* I wondered if God would see this as a selfish thing for me to do.

I broached the subject with Ken, and his response reassured me. "God made this world, and I believe He wants us to enjoy it."

For some of us, I would come to realize, exploring the extraordinary parts of this world is one of the most meaningful ways to enjoy God's creation.

When we finished our lunch break, we headed down the ridge to the top of a steep snowfield. We could see our trail far below. Near the top of the slope, we found a big groove in the snow that previous hikers had made by sliding down to the bottom of the hill. It reminded me of a toboggan run.

"That's where we're going," Ken gestured toward it with a grin.

I looked at the chute with alarm. All I could think about was the possibility of catching my foot on the slide down and tearing my ACL again. "I don't know if I can do that," I said meekly.

This is how Bob and Ken introduced me to another fun aspect of climbing—the sitting glissade! This involves sitting in the snow and sliding down the slope, using an ice axe to control your speed. On many snow-covered slopes in the mountains, it is possible to find a sliding path already set in the snow, just like we'd done. This makes the descent faster and more exciting.

"Before we slide down that, we'll teach you how to do a self-arrest with your ice axe," Bob assured me. "You can't climb on a glaciated peak like Mount Rainier unless you know how to do this. You *have* to be able to stop yourself if you fall."

Ken placed his ice axe across his body. "Grab the head like this," he said, showing us what he meant, "and put your hand toward the bottom of the shaft. Hold the top of the axe near one shoulder, and the bottom near your opposite hip."

"Are you going to demonstrate?" Bob asked. "Or shall I?"

"I'll do it." Ken threw himself down the snowy slope, turned himself onto his stomach as he slid, and thrust the pick of his axe into the ice until his body came to a stop.

"You have to learn how to do it from any position you find yourself in when you fall," Bob said. "Now it's your turn."

John and I took turns throwing ourselves down the snow-field several times, sometimes diving headfirst, other times falling on our sides. Our teachers encouraged us when we did it right, and gave us tips to correct what we did wrong. Once we all felt comfortable with John's and my results, we headed toward the snow chute.

The three-foot-deep toboggan run we faced just begged to be tackled. Ken went first, then I sat down to take my turn.

I hesitated. "I don't know," I said, still not convinced it was a good idea.

"You'll be fine." Bob patted my shoulder.

"You'll be able to control the speed of your slide with the ice axe," Ken shouted from below.

I sat down and pushed myself over the lip of the slope. Even though I held the point of my axe along my side and shoved it into the snow the whole way, I rapidly gained speed. Then I slowed as a pile of soft snow built up in front of my feet, and I pushed it down ahead of me. I descended at a considerably slower pace than Ken had before me. At the bottom, I decided the slide hadn't scared me as much as I thought it would. Next time, I would let myself go faster.

After this first outing, I felt pretty good about my readiness for our Mount Rainier climb.

On an afternoon in early June, I headed down to Centralia for our trip to Mount St. Helens. Ken's wife, Jeannie, fixed me a cot in their family room, where I slept for only a few hours. We got up at five o'clock in the morning so we could get to the trailhead and start early in the day.

Though I didn't know it at the time, our climb that day was my introduction to the active volcano that I would return to every year for the next twelve years. The climb up St. Helens would become an integral part of my training regimen.

We parked in the lot at the trailhead where we met up with Ken's friends. Once we hit the trail, I settled into a comfortable rhythm. The path started in the forest, but before long it reached timberline, where trees no longer could grow. That's where we entered the zone of snow and rocks. As we ascended, heat from the bright sun overhead drove away the morning chill. The glare of sunshine reflecting off the surface of the snow further intensified the heat and the bright sunlight. I took off my long pants and climbed in shorts, sweating freely while plodding up the snowy slope in the steps made by earlier climbers.

As we moved steadily up the snowfields, I experienced for the first time the hypnotic effect of placing my feet one step at a time in footprints that led interminably uphill. Sometimes I passed other hikers from our own group or other groups and felt a sense of satisfaction. Other times hikers passed me. This reminded me that I wasn't the strongest climber on the slope. Even so, I felt satisfied with my conditioning.

A few times, following a rest break, I started off after John had already headed up the mountain. Each time I slowly caught up. When he heard me approaching, he stepped aside, off the trail. "You go ahead," he panted.

Each time, I took in his red face and listened to his labored breathing.

"Thanks," I replied as I stepped past. I needed to keep going to maintain the comfortable, rhythmic pace that worked best for me. Each time, his heavy breathing followed me until I drew far enough away for the sound to fade.

The climb that day introduced me to the smell of sweat and sunscreen combined with the need to take in measured, steady breaths of thin air, all while climbing under a boundless sapphire sky. These odors and actions would become my constant companions in the years to come. One sniff of sunscreen on my pack straps as I warm up brings back a flood of memories.

Finally, I reached a place where I could take no more upward steps. The slope eased off, and as climbers reached the summit, we carefully peered over the edge to check out the lava dome nestled in St. Helens' crater. We didn't dare approach too closely, since it looked like a lip of snow hung out over the edge. The cornice perched over a cliff that plunged 1,000 feet to the floor of the crater below. Mount Rainier sat on the horizon to the north. The towering white bulk of Mount Adams dominated the view to the east. I marveled at the breathtaking panorama.

Ken had reached the top before me. I handed him my camera and he took the obligatory summit photos for me. From my pack, I pulled out an insulating pad that kept me off the snow. Looking around, I found a place to sit near the rim of the crater. I delighted in the gorgeous blue sky. Then I searched in my pack for my lunch. A young man and woman who'd just reached the top settled down on the snow a few feet away to my right. They glanced at my bare legs and one of them said, "That's quite the scar there. Did you have an ACL repaired?"

I looked at the two long scars on either side of my knee. It impressed me that they recognized the source. "Yeah, how did you know?"

They explained that they were both nurses. "How long ago did you have your surgery?" the man asked.

I told them about the initial surgery sixteen months before and the follow-up in November.

"It's really great that you made this climb. Congratulations!" the woman exclaimed.

The guy reached into his pack and pulled out a flask. He held it out to me. "We're going to celebrate our success with a sip of brandy. Would you like to join us?"

I was flattered, but their offer didn't tempt me. I turned them down but thanked them for the encouragement.

Ken and John settled down a few feet away on my other side. I overheard a sweat-soaked John tell Ken, "I'm just not doing good with this. The climb up was a real struggle for me."

This didn't surprise me.

"I just don't think I'm ready for Rainier," he said.

"You're doing okay," Ken tried to encourage him. "You still have two weeks to train."

"I'm just not going to be in shape for it," John insisted. With that, our little climbing team shrank to three.

Descending the mountain was a whole lot more fun than climbing up had been—and it took a lot less time. We glissaded more than halfway down by sliding through several snow-fields. At the bottom of each, we walked to the left, to the top of the next snowfield to keep on track. Repeat, all the way to the tree line.

The more elevation we lost, the faster I let myself slide. The snow, soft from sunshine, and the perfect angle of the slope kept me from going too fast for comfort. I fell in love with glissading!

When we reached the parking lot, I took stock. My mus-cles felt stronger than ever before. I had lost all the weight I'd gained while being inactive, and a little more. I now had all the climbing skills I would need to make a summit attempt.

I knew I was ready for Mount Rainier.

THE CLIMB

Ich kann nicht mehr.
(I can't anymore.)

—Toni Kurz, mountaineer, while trapped
on the north face of the Eiger, 1936

I met Ken and Bob midmorning in the parking lot at Paradise, a popular tourist destination where the nearby visitors' lodge sits at the foot of Mount Rainier, at an elevation of 5,400 feet.

After some quick last-minute organizing, we donned our packs. Bob helped me lift mine to my back. I'd left the days of twenty-five and thirty-pound packs behind me since I now had to carry the extra gear needed for climbing, including crampons, a harness, and several carabiners.

We took off uphill through snow-covered meadows under a cerulean sky unsullied by clouds. Ahead, the many tracks of climbers who'd tackled the hill earlier came together to form a trail.

Bob pointed out landmarks along the way. "There's a vista point over there." And, "That's Panorama Point up there. We're headed for that."

I craned my head up to look at the daunting heights. The icy, gleaming cone of Mount Rainier taunted us.

After a couple of hours, we topped out on a small rise and checked out a depression in front of us. Water rushed from underneath the snow to our right, gurgled through a rocky bed, then plunged over a steep drop to our left.

"This is Pebble Creek," Bob said. "It means we're about halfway to Camp Muir."

We planned to stay the night at the climbers' camp.

"Should we take a lunch break?" Ken suggested.

"Sure," I said with enthusiasm. After all the exertion, I welcomed the chance to eat something. I also felt the beginnings of a headache.

"I think it's a great idea," Bob agreed.

We settled on dark rocks near an icy stream of water. White froth formed behind small stones, then sent bubbles floating on the current toward the valley below.

We pulled out our lunch bags, and I found my salt tablets. The wet stains on my shirt attested to how much liquid I'd sweated out. *Maybe the salt will help my headache,* I thought.

Soon two men approached, climbing toward us from below. They wore gear similar to ours—synthetic long-sleeved shirts, rugged pants, and heavy boots.

"Where are you headed?" Bob asked the one in front.

"Camp Muir," the man answered.

"Are you going to try to climb the mountain?" Bob asked.

"Yeah, we're planning to take off tonight," he said as he passed by.

"So are we," Ken said.

"Good luck," the trailing hiker offered.

"You, too," said Ken.

The last slog up the Muir Snowfield below Camp Muir took everything I had. We had been climbing for over six hours. Up ahead I could see what looked like a square pile of rocks from almost a mile down the snowfield. This was the climbing hut—our goal. A tall, narrow wooden structure—the outhouse—sat nearby. But no matter how many steps we slowly took up the slope, we never seemed to draw any closer.

About halfway up the snowfield, we reached Anvil Rock, a craggy point on the ridge off to the right. We sat down nearby on some dark rocks in a snow-free patch. It was time to try to choke some food down and drink some water.

I eyed my gorp warily. Even the chocolate chips didn't appeal to me. I took a few bites of a granola bar. My headache had grown no worse, and perhaps even receded a little. The salt tablets I took at Pebble Creek appeared to have helped.

Before long, Ken spoke up. "We better get going. It's getting late."

"Let's do this last stretch without stopping," Bob suggested.

Ken helped me lift my pack to my back and when we were ready, Bob took the lead. I fell into last place. Step—breathe—step—breathe. I fell into the rhythm of pacing myself, a newly learned skill. Moving up the snowy slope still felt like the hardest thing I had ever done. A gap widened between the two men and me. We could see the goal ahead and there was no danger that anyone would get lost. We just had to get there.

A few minutes after they reached the saddle where Camp Muir sat, I approached the last steep steps that led up to a flat area formed by dirt, surrounded by rocks, and covered with snow and tracks. Several feet back from the edge, I spotted a tall, lanky man. At first glance I thought it was Ken, but after a second look I realized someone else stood there, someone who looked vaguely familiar.

Step—breathe—step—breathe—five more steps to go. Four more. Three. Then the last two and I stepped onto the surface of my goal. I stopped to catch my breath. I looked at the tall man and he gave me a big smile. "Welcome to Camp Muir," he greeted me enthusiastically.

When I heard his deep voice, the man's identity dawned on me. I couldn't say anything. Lou Whittaker stood before me. Lou Whittaker, the famous climber whose twin brother, Jim, had been the first American to reach the summit of Mount Everest, in 1963. Lou Whittaker, the owner of Rainier Mountaineering, Inc., the only guide service to lead climbs on Mount Rainier at that time. In the climbing world, he stood near the top.

I found a remnant of my voice as my breathing grew easier. "Thanks," I mumbled. Then he turned and joined several people by a small wooden hut to the left. Park rangers used this hut, and the guide service also parked clients in there.

Later, after I had settled into camp, I met a couple of people in Lou's climbing party. I learned that he had accompanied a group of employees of the outdoor gear company JanSport on their summit attempt that week. *Did he think I was one of them? Or is he this friendly to everyone?* It didn't matter to me. I had been welcomed to Camp Muir by Lou Whittaker!

I checked my watch—almost four o'clock on the dot. I saw Bob's sturdy figure coming toward me as Ken emerged from the outhouse. Bob gestured to the stone hut behind him. "There's a lot of snow up here," he said. "We'll have to climb into the hut."

As we approached, I saw that the bottom of the door was buried in snow. Only the upper half was accessible.

"It's split like a Dutch door," Bob pointed out. "We'll need to climb through the top half and drop down to the floor."

Everything I had seen and experienced since the first couple of hours of our climb had felt foreign and unfamiliar. The task of struggling under a heavy pack, surrounded by a stark environment of icy snow, black rocks, and cold wind, was too much to completely grasp. I had found myself focusing on one task and then the next. I took off my pack and went to use the cold out-house, then came back and followed Bob and Ken into the hut.

After I passed my pack down to Ken, he helped me slide through the door down to the cement floor. The chilled air struck me first. It was so cold that it felt like being inside a refrigerator. Next, I noticed the earthy aroma of stones and dirt and sweaty clothes, and under those, the cloying odor of burned stove fuel.

I looked around what felt like an unlit cave. Ahead of me, two levels of bunks butted up against the right wall. But they weren't single bunks, I realized. I peered into the darkness. Lumps of sleeping-bag-wrapped climbers lay side by side on solid plywood platforms that extended as far back as I could see.

On my left, a waist-high wooden counter stretched the length of the wall. Stoves and gas bottles and gear-related odds and ends were indistinct in the gloom. Between the bunks and the shelf, a narrow passageway led to the back wall.

I started to say something to Ken and heard a *shush* com-ing from the closest bunk. "There are people trying to sleep in here," said a quiet voice.

Bob emerged from the darkness at the other end of the hut. "There's a place on the top bunk back there where we can all fit," he whispered.

Ken and I followed him back and tossed our gear onto our chosen spots. Before climbing into our sleeping bags for a few hours of sleep, we melted snow on our gas stove, contributing to the polluted atmosphere, and replenished our water. Then we focused on food. My appetite was destroyed by exhaus-tion and altitude, but I choked down my freeze-dried beef and potatoes.

"Is that any good?" Bob asked, as he sliced a piece of sum-mer sausage off a hunk he carried. His ramen sat nearby in his camp cup.

"It's okay," I said. The potatoes tasted like cardboard.

Soon, it was time to crawl into our sleeping bags. New, alien experiences conspired to keep me awake: Lying in a cold stone hut on a wooden bunk with only a thin foam pad for comfort. Listening to the soft breathing and snores of a dozen other people, probably all men. Curling up in my sleeping bag, gathering it around me to fight the cold.

I finally dropped into a restless sleep. Very little time passed before I awoke to the music of carabiners jingling and the soft voices of a new team of climbers coming into the hut. I listened as they followed the same routine we had—soft voices discussing where to sleep, a hissing stove as they fixed food and melted water, and finally thumps and groans as they settled into their sleeping bags. Then it grew quiet again. I would soon learn what it meant to start an ascent on just three or four hours of sleep.

It seemed like my eyes had been closed for only a few minutes when I woke to movement on one side of me. Bob sat up in his sleeping bag and I peeked at him from mine, pulled tight around my face. He pulled a warm wool shirt over his head and readied himself to climb down from the bunk.

"Time to get up," he whispered. "It's midnight, and we want to get climbing by one o'clock."

I felt Ken moving on my other side and picked up the sounds of people rustling and moving in the dark. I reluctantly pulled on a second shirt over my first layer, then pulled my long-underwear-clad legs out of my sleeping bag and slipped them into my wool pants.

I was proud of my pants. Ken had warned me about spending too much money on gear and clothing for an experience that might never be repeated. I had borrowed, rented, and spent judiciously to cover my needs. The pants were my tour de force. I had scoured an Army Navy surplus store and found a pair of navy-blue wool dress pants—just like those in my mother's cedar chest. They had been part of my father's uniform when he served in the US Navy! My pants felt thick and promised warmth.

There was one problem—to pull them on, I'd originally had to open a front panel that closed with thirteen buttons. Thirteen! I knew I wouldn't want to deal with thirteen buttons, or even ten, while up on the mountain with thick gloves or cold fingers and who knew how much wind. So, in preparation, I'd taken the buttons off one side of the panel and sewed Velcro in place to keep it closed. This solution worked great. Except for one problem. When taking my pants off in the hut before climbing into bed, the scratchy noise reminded me just how loud Velcro sounds when you rip it apart. Sorry, guys!

We heated water for breakfast and topped off our bottles. Then we sorted our gear and got ready to put everything we'd need for our summit attempt into one pack.

"I think we should use my pack," I said.

Ken and Bob looked it over with skepticism. The new style of pack I carried had an internal frame and was only recently catching on with climbers.

"I borrowed it from my physical therapist, and he says it's easier to carry than the old frame packs you guys have."

"We can give it a try," Ken said.

Bob found a place to stash their packs while we climbed.

We gathered our climbing gear and the pack and clambered out the door into the cold, inky darkness punctuated by pools of light from climbers' headlamps. We all wore extra layers. I pulled on a wool hat with a picture of a team of huskies knitted into it, then gathered my long brown hair into a ponytail. Bob's hat covered his thin gray hair, while Ken's protected the bare scalp peeking through his close-cropped russet hair.

A sweep of a headlamp revealed several climbers sitting on scattered rocks around the camp. Others stood on the edge of the nearby glacier, working to spread out their ropes. Bob,

Ken, and I found our own rocks to perch on and strapped our crampons onto our boots.

The time I'd spent practicing with my crampons now paid off. A tricky pattern of crisscrossing the straps across the boots needed to be done accurately. If the crampons didn't remain securely attached, the consequences could be deadly. I had made sure I knew how to do it at home, and had even worn my boots and crampons around my backyard.

"I practiced walking with them," I joked while strapping them on. "I aerated our lawn."

Bob spread our rope out across the edge of the Cowlitz Glacier just beyond camp. He coiled nearly a third of it for carrying, so we wouldn't be climbing too far apart. Then he tied a knot with a loop near the coil and another in the middle of the stretched-out portion of rope for the middle person.

"We'll put you in the middle," he said to me, "since you're the least experienced. I'll lead first and Ken will be in back. He and I will trade off later."

Ken pulled the pack onto his tall, spare frame and tied in to the end of the rope. Bob picked up the extra coil of rope, and he and I used sturdy carabiners to attach our climbing harnesses to the pretied loops.

Bob turned around. "Are you ready?"

I looked into the darkness ahead, snow gleaming in the cone of light from my headlamp. "I guess so," I said, even though tension rose in my throat. I wasn't at all sure that I could conquer the challenge ahead.

"Yep," Ken said, and Bob led out across the Cowlitz Glacier toward Cathedral Gap. The glacier crossing was easier than I expected, lulling me into feeling confident early on. The trail advanced with a moderate vertical rise and we didn't encounter any crevasses.

In less than half an hour we reached the small ridge known as Cathedral Rocks. I followed Bob onto a surface of small rocks and dirt where we crossed a low spot in the ridge. The experience of walking on rocks in crampons slowed me down, and I wondered if I would damage them by walking on the uneven surface. Bob barely slowed, so I figured out how to navigate the uneven ground on the little spikes. Wearing crampons had seemed so much easier when they just had to bite into snow.

Before long we dropped down onto another glacier—the Ingraham Glacier. We went uphill and followed the base of the ridge we had just crossed. The slope soon eased off and Bob pointed ahead to a wide, gently sloping area on the glacier.

"That's called Ingraham Flats," he said. "We're going to cross that. Sometimes people come all the way up here to camp on the first day. Or sometimes they camp below Camp Muir, then come here and camp again before they make their summit attempt."

That sounds like an easier way to do it, I thought.

When we reached the Flats, we took a rest break. Bob and Ken huddled together to talk about the route ahead. They examined the slopes above, pointing and talking, while deciding what to do next.

Finally, Ken turned to me. "Usually, we would cut over to the right and cross at the bottom of Disappointment Cleaver." He pointed. "Then the route follows the Cleaver up to there." He indicated a spot about halfway to the top.

"But, we're going to do the Ingraham Direct route today. It looks like all the crevasses that open up later in the season are still buried. There was plenty of snow this winter, and the weather's been cool all spring, so most of it hasn't melted."

"That means we're going to go straight up the glacier." Bob pointed up the slope. "Then we'll cut over to the right, to the top of Disappointment Cleaver. From there we'll probably follow the standard route. We'll check it out when we get to the top of the Cleaver."

As Ken and Bob talked, I looked up the slope, oblivious to what their plan meant. *If they say this is the way to go, then so be it.*

We worked our way across the Flats and started up the steep slope beyond it, climbing under a clear robin's egg sky. The sun hadn't risen far above the horizon, but it promised to bathe us in its harsh glare all day long.

Halfway up the slope to the top of the Cleaver, we took another break. I sat down beside Ken and thrust my ice axe into the snow.

"Ow!" he exclaimed. "Watch out!" I looked down and saw that the sharp end of my axe pick had caught his wool pants, torn them slightly, and scratched his leg underneath.

I grimaced. "I'm sorry," I said with chagrin. "I need to be more careful."

"That's okay," he assured me. "It's not too bad." Nevertheless, I apologized again. *I have to think about every move I make up here,* I thought.

I sat munching on a snack and looked down the steep glacier. I could see all the way down the icy slope to the tree-covered hills 5,000 feet below. *In this world, everything is down,* I thought. *Any misstep and something will go plunging downhill.* I took a drink of water and very carefully set my water bottle down in a small divot in the snow so it wouldn't go rolling and bouncing down to the forests below.

Before we set out again, I took advantage of a trick the guys had taught me. I dug down through the icy crust to clean snow, scooped it up, and refilled my bottle. After a little while, the water remaining in the bottle would melt the snow and replenish the liquid we greedily drank at each rest stop. In the meantime, each sip tasted ice-cold.

Bob took his turn carrying the pack and Ken led the next leg of the climb. Soon Bob called out, "Let's stop a minute. This pack is really uncomfortable."

I knew they made different sizes to fit different heights of people. *Is the pack too short for him?* I wondered.

"Tighten up the waist belt and loosen the shoulder straps so you're carrying more of the weight on your hips," I called down. My therapist had described this sort of adjustment. Bob did his best to follow my suggestion and it seemed to relieve most of the strain on his shoulders.

When we reached a point on the slope where we approached the same elevation as the top of the Cleaver, Ken started angling toward his goal. To get there, we skirted a monstrous crevasse. It was my first encounter with one of these yawning turquoise holes. Ken approached the gaping blue fissure in the snow, then led us across a wide snowbridge between two bottomless clefts. Then he continued his traverse up the steep slope above us. I had to stop to take a picture. I'd read all about crevasses, but here, in person, I actually saw the beauty and sensed the potential danger. *I'm really here.*

Not far beyond the crevasse, we reached a spot where the angle of the slope briefly eased. Now that we had arrived at the top of the Cleaver, we needed to choke down some food, take stock, and decide our next moves. The view above the summit had morphed from a clear sapphire sky into a cloud cap. This lens-shaped, lenticular cloud obscured the top of the mountain and portended a change in the weather.

Ken looked at it. "Even if we summit, we're not going to have much of a view."

"We'll still be able to say we made it to the top," Bob said. "Are you two still feeling okay?"

We both said we were fine.

"Then let's keep going. We'll go off to the right to avoid those two big crevasses." Bob pointed up the slope. "Then we can go back to the left and up to the summit."

We soon headed up again. Though I moved almost on autopilot, a steady undercurrent of doubt took up residence in my mind. *Can I make it all the way? If we go all the way to the top, will my knee stand up to the long downhill trek?* I knew that getting to the top was only half the journey. I needed to finish the second half, too.

On our ascent we passed other climbing groups, all headed down. No one else was still going up. We had the mountain to ourselves.

The breeze picked up as we drew closer to the cloud cover. Then the fog enveloped us and the wind blew even harder. Our world shrank to a steep icy slope, a few tracks in the snow, and the dark outlines of our team members. As I followed Bob up the trail through the hard snow, wind gusts buffeted me sideways and backward. I felt like I took one step back for every two steps up.

I stopped a couple of times and we huddled together.

"We're almost there," Bob assured me each time. "Just a little farther."

"You can do it," Ken said.

Finally, the fear took over. I stopped. "I don't think I can go anymore," I said. I looked up into the gray veil, not knowing if the top was thirty steps up, or three hundred.

Bob examined my face, trying to assess my state of mind. He and Ken conferred and decided they wouldn't push me any further.

We took our summit pictures sitting in the snow and leaning uphill into the slope. Bob's smile looked more genuine than mine. After a short rest, our little climbing group headed back the way we had come.

The route that had been so hard going up seemed to fly by going down. As soon as we dropped below the influence of the cloud cap, the wind calmed and the sun took over. Before long, we started peeling off layers of shirts and jackets so we wouldn't overheat. At a short stop, I looked back up the slope toward the summit above. The cloud had disappeared.

"Look." I pointed up. "It's clear!"

If only I had been willing to keep going. Maybe I would have been fine coming down. Maybe I should have just pushed a little longer.

"Yeah," Ken said a bit wistfully.

"The wind up there is probably still howling," Bob said.

Though disappointed, I knew the decision to come down was final. We couldn't head back up now.

We slogged through softening snow, the heat of the sun lulling me into a daze. Under the sun's glare, the top layer of firm snow had turned to mush that grabbed our feet. We reached the bottom of the steep slope and started across Ingraham Flats.

Bob walked ahead of me as we stepped in turn across a couple of small crevasses that were barely open. Each of us called out "Crossing" whenever we reached one and stepped or jumped across.

Suddenly, I saw something that jolted me out of my complacency: I noticed Bob make a funny lurching step. Without breaking his stride, he called, "Watch out through there," and continued on.

I followed his tracks in the snow and when I reached the area where he had stumbled, I saw the cause. A perfect cookie-cutter boot shape went through six inches of snow, and a bottomless hole showed only blue darkness below. Bob must have punched through the soft surface layer.

I took a big jump before I reached the track, making sure to land a good distance beyond it. *Just how wide is that crevasse?* I certainly didn't want to find out.

I turned around to warn Ken. He made it through with no problems.

We continued our descent, retracing our upward route. When we reached Camp Muir, we unroped. I took off my crampons while Bob coiled the rope into a package that could be strapped to his pack. Then we gathered the gear we had cached in the hut and headed down the Muir Snowfield. Our plan included one more night on the mountain. Exhaustion overwhelmed us after our long day, and as evening approached, we didn't want to undertake the grueling trip down to Paradise.

Instead of staying the night in the hut at Camp Muir, however, the guys decided to descend five hundred feet in elevation and set up a camp near Anvil Rock. It took us less than fifteen minutes to reach a relatively flat spot. I perched on a nearby rock to rest and shook out my sweaty hair. I watched Ken and Bob flatten an area of snow big enough to set up Ken's little orange camping tent. They faced the door of the tent downhill, which gave us a great panoramic view of the valley below when we peeked out.

We went through the now-familiar routine of melting snow, fixing dinner, and topping off our water bottles.

We sat with our food in our laps. This time it was Ken who asked, "How do you like that freeze-dried dinner?"

I choked down a bite of beef and potatoes. "I'm not impressed."

He and Bob laughed as they enjoyed their second night of ramen with sausage and cheese.

We soon climbed into our sleeping bags. I had never camped on snow before. The two men sandwiched me between them. Even with their body heat close by, fingers of cold air still snuck in to chill me around the edges. My long underwear and summer-weight sleeping bag didn't provide enough insulation. Still, I managed to doze off. I woke up every so often and took a big gulp of water from the bottle I'd stashed near my head. I craved the liquid after all the sweating I'd done throughout a long day of climbing.

Near midnight, something other than my thirst woke me. A breeze sighed over the tent and caused a flapping sound as it caught the loose, nylon door. Soon, the percussion of flapping and slapping provided a drumbeat for the soft sough of the wind.

First Ken, and then Bob, woke up as the southwest wind strengthened. Strong gusts pushed at regular intervals against one side of the tent, deforming its symmetrical shape. The wind we'd felt near the summit now reached down to buffet us in our campsite. The gusts began pushing the roof toward our noses as we lay in our protective cocoons.

After a particularly violent blast, Ken asked Bob in alarm, "How well did you stake the corners of the tent?"

"Not well enough," Bob said. "This is getting pretty bad."

Bob wormed his way out of his sleeping bag, pulled on pants and a coat, and grabbed a headlamp. He opened the tent door at our feet, letting in a rush of cold air, and thrust his feet into his boots. The time had come to face the gale.

He crawled out into the maelstrom and gathered together our ice axes. One by one, he drove two of them into the snow near the windward corners of the tent and tied the tent securely to their shafts. He did the same with the third axe on the far side of the tent door. Satisfied, he crawled back inside to escape the wind.

We lay there listening to the howl of the gale and watching the nylon wall approach within inches of our faces. "This is just a backpacking tent," Ken said. "I don't think it's meant to take this kind of wind." He could already tell the tent's poles were bowing as they surrendered to the power of the rushing torrent of air.

The howling wind offered no mercy as the black sky gave way to a blanket of gray. The lenticular cloud capping Rainier's summit during our climb had given us fair warning of this storm. We had ignored the omen. Now we felt the full strength of the storm's fury.

When darkness finally gave way to cloudy daylight, we crawled out of the tent.

"Let's not try to get the stove lit and fix breakfast," Bob suggested. "We can eat a few snacks and ration the water in our bottles. After we get off the mountain, we can stop in Eatonville for a real breakfast."

"That sounds good to me," Ken agreed. "I could go for bacon and eggs and hash browns."

I realized that my appetite was coming back. Having breakfast together sounded like a great way to top off our experience before the men headed back to Centralia and I took off north toward home.

"I like that idea," I said. "Except I want sausage."

We packed up as efficiently as we could, taking care not to let anything fly away in the teeth of the wind. Ken and Bob dismantled the tent. As Bob folded the nylon body, Ken gathered up the poles. "I don't know if I will ever be able to use these again." He held out a couple of the aluminum poles to show their new rainbow curves. Indeed, the tent hadn't been designed for the severe conditions we'd experienced.

Once we were packed, we charged down the mountain, each step a long, plunging thrust that broke through icy crust into soft snow underneath. My mind stayed on autopilot as I followed Ken and Bob. With the loss of elevation, the speed and ferocity of the wind eased. It took us considerably less time to get down than it had taken to climb up to Camp Muir just two days before.

When we reached the parking lot, tremendous relief flooded through me as I eased my pack off for the last time. The warm restroom beckoned and I headed over with an armful of clean, dry clothes. The promised breakfast called to me. During the climb, I'd had to force myself to eat, but now I had a huge appetite.

I followed Bob and Ken to Eatonville in my own car. We pulled into the parking lot of a little restaurant on the corner of the main intersection. I sat across from Bob, enjoying his mature smiling face. Ken's grin livened his freckled skin, rosy from sun and wind.

We shared our thoughts about the expedition over bacon and sausage and eggs and hash browns. No guilt.

I already recognized in myself an urge to go back, to actually touch the official summit—and to face the thrill of cheating danger.

"I talked to the ranger when I checked us out," Bob told us. "When I described where we'd turned around, he agreed we could count it as a successful summit. He put it in his records that way."

I mulled that over. The book showed our climb as a success. But in my heart, I felt like I had unfinished business to take care of.

GLACIER BASIN

For observing nature, the best
pace is a snail's pace.

—Edwin Way Teale

"Hey, little guy." I caught my youngest son's attention.

"What, Mom?" Tim looked at me, his dark-chocolate eyes full of trust. I smiled at his tanned little face with the dimple on his right cheek.

"You know, I took Kris backpacking two years ago, and he and I are going to hike to Mystic Lake in a few weeks. How would you like to go on your first backpacking trip before that?"

"I don't know if I can do it," he said. I was looking for a smile that would cause the dimple to appear, but his expression was one of apprehension.

I looked at his slim figure, his head topped with brown hair, straight bangs falling over his forehead. He was almost the same age as his older brother had been when I took him with me to Lake Ann. He was as tall as Kris had been at the same age, but his slender body weighed several pounds less. On the plus side, he always displayed lots of energy. "The trail's not very long," I said. "And you won't have to carry much. Maybe just your jacket and your lunch."

"Okay," he tentatively agreed.

Blue skies blessed us as we donned our packs in the parking lot near Mount Rainier two weeks later.

After climbing Rainier in June, I realized I was strong enough to carry all of the camping gear I would need for Tim's first backpacking trip. I'd picked Glacier Basin in Mount Rainier National Park for our adventure. Ken had told me about an alternate climbing route through the basin during the summit attempt we'd made following the Muir route. The trail guide's description said the campsites were only a little over three miles from the parking lot. Surely a distance short enough for a six-year-old.

We started toward the Glacier Basin trail. Tim wore a little day pack and I had an overloaded frame pack, with a tent and sleeping bag strapped to the outside. A sign beside the trailhead described some of the history of the area. Faded pictures showed old buildings and mining scenes.

"Look, Tim." I pointed to one of the pictures. "It says that people used to mine up here a long time ago."

"Let's go." He started up the trail, not at all interested in history. I followed.

Before long, I heard those words every parent dreads: "How far is it, Mom?"

"A little over three miles. That's really not very far," I reassured him.

Sometimes I led the way, adjusting my pace to Tim's short legs. Sometimes I urged him to walk in front so I could keep an eye on him.

We had hiked almost a mile when he asked, "When are we going to stop?"

"There's a good place just ahead." Within a couple of minutes, we reached an intersection with the Emmons Vista trail that took off toward the Emmons Glacier.

"Let's take a break here," I suggested.

We found rocks to sit on beside the trail. "You can have a snack if you want," I said.

He searched his pack for a snack bag, the only thing he carried besides his jacket, and found a candy bar.

We watched several other hikers pass while we rested, some with packs on their backs.

Hiking another half mile took us to the middle of a dense forest of old-growth trees, where we stopped again. As we sat on a log, we watched several men approach from the mountain. They tromped toward us in big boots, their packs bristling with crampons and ropes and tent poles.

"Look." I gestured toward them. "Those guys are mountain climbers."

His eyes widened.

"Hi," I said to the first man in the group. His hair was disheveled and he wore a long-sleeved polypropylene shirt pushed up to his shoulders. His face showed fatigue under a dark tan. "How was your climb?"

"It was good," he said without stopping.

"Did you summit?" I asked.

The second in line, a man wearing a white hat, responded with a tired smile. "Yeah, we got to the top about six thirty this morning."

The four men kept moving down the trail with determined strides, so I just called to their backs, "Congratulations! Have a good hike out."

"Thanks." The last man in line tossed me this small conversational bone.

Soon after we started up again, Tim and I emerged from the forest. A spectacular view of the valley and our first glimpse of Mount Rainier opened up before us. About fifteen minutes later we crossed a small stream burbling down from the forested ridge on our right. We noticed some rusty machinery beside the trail. "What's this?" Tim asked. He pointed to a huge rusty metal gear, about two to three feet in diameter, emerging from the dirt and undergrowth on the uphill side of the trail.

"That's from those mines I mentioned," I told him. "Miners were looking for copper in Glacier Basin."

The gear was planted firmly in the soil. I guessed that it had to weigh at least a couple hundred pounds. Still, in subsequent years as I continued to hike this trail, I watched as the artifact worked its way from the uphill side of the trail to the downhill side. Then one year, I realized it was nowhere to be found, having finally disappeared into the trees on the steep slope below.

Tim and I slowed down when we reached the last half mile of the trail. It made up the steepest part of the hike. When I saw an old telephone pole leaning on the slope above, planted in a green meadow sprinkled with flowers, I knew we would reach the campsite shortly. "Just a little bit more," I reassured Tim.

Within a couple of minutes, we spotted the camp sign beside the trail. Just beyond it was a short post with the number 5 engraved on it, sticking up beside a beaten trail leading into the trees on the right. We followed the path for a few yards and found a flat, bare spot whose perimeter was lined by logs to mark the camping area.

"What do you think?" I asked. "Those logs look good enough to sit on. And look over there. That flat rock will be a great place to set up our stove."

"I guess." Tim still seemed hesitant to give himself fully to the adventure.

We thankfully shrugged off our packs and set them against a log, claiming our site.

I wanted to check out the rest of the area. "Come on, Tim. Let's go see the meadow."

We left our packs and walked through the camp, following the trail toward the treeless meadow beyond the campground. Just before we reached the grassy expanse, on our right we noticed a large rectangular hole in the ground, strewn with angular rocks.

"What's that?" Tim asked.

"I'm not sure."

We continued the short distance to the edge of the camp area and took in the scene. The whole basin spread out ahead of us.

To our left, a rushing creek flowed through a broad, rocky valley bottom. Beyond that, a steep rock-strewn ridge rose to a point: Mount Ruth. The bottom of Inter Glacier peeked out from behind Mount Ruth. Straight ahead, a ridge started at a small rocky saddle and extended toward the right. Its crest was made of steep jagged rocks that marched up to a barren rock buttress composed of columnar basalt. A partially tree-covered slope fell from the buttress all the way down to the meadow in front of us. It was hard to take in the grandeur of it all.

Tim and I headed back to the campsites, which were huddled in the trees on a flat shelf below a small knoll and above the rocky valley floor. A sign that read "Toilet" pointed toward a narrow trail that led up the knoll and through the trees. The trail ended at a box toilet perched in a small space carved out of the forest. Just like the toilet Kris and I had used on our trip to Lake Ann, it was best used when someone stood guard several yards down the trail.

We continued to explore a little and found a narrow trail that wandered toward the buttress ridge. It skirted the edge of a shallow pond taking up one corner of the meadow. The pond was nestled against the slope below the buttress.

As we passed the pond, Tim suddenly knelt down. "Look, Mom," he said excitedly. "Frogs!"

I looked where he pointed and saw movement. "I see them! And look at those little black things swimming around. Those are tadpoles."

He spent several minutes watching them, while I looked around. Then I found one of my favorite wildflowers.

"Look at these, Tim." I beckoned. "See these little blossoms?" A bouquet of purple flowerlets lined the stalk. "Don't they look just like the head of an elephant?"

He peered at where I pointed. "Yeah, they do," he agreed.

"That's why they're called elephants-head," I explained.

It was the first time I had seen these since I lived in Colorado during college and spent time in the Rocky Mountains, over twelve years earlier. I was thrilled to find this fanciful purple flower.

We wandered back to our camp and set up our little orange A-frame tent. Before long, a tall young lady approached, with long brown hair falling below her shoulders. She wore dark-green wool shorts and a shirt the same color gray as worn by the Park Service.

"Hi. My name is Jenny Knauer," she said with a big smile and an East Coast accent.

"Are you from around here?" I asked.

"I came here all the way from New Jersey to be a volunteer ranger with the Student Conservation Association."

I introduced Tim and myself. "We're up here to camp for a couple of nights. It's Tim's first backpacking trip."

"That's great!" she said. "It's nice to see someone so young being introduced to the joys of the wilderness. Did you get a permit at the ranger station?"

"Sure did," I replied. "It's over there, attached to our tent."

"Great." She took a quick look at it. "Two nights, huh?"

"Yep. That'll give us time for exploring."

I had never met student volunteers before. "What's your job here?"

"When I'm up here, I patrol the Glacier Basin area and check camping permits, answer hikers' questions, and make sure they know the wilderness rules. Like 'don't step off the trail.'" She pointed to a man and woman walking through the grass in the meadow. "That's really hard on the vegetation, and we do everything we can to discourage it."

"Let's talk more later," she said, then took off toward the couple in the meadow.

As evening approached, Jenny indeed came back to our camp. She suggested, "Why don't you come out to the meadow with me? We might see some mountain goats."

"Mountain goats?" Tim asked with his eyes wide open. He quickly stood up to follow.

As we trailed Jenny through camp, she paused at the big hole in the ground. Gesturing, she said, "That's where an old hotel stood when the coal miners were up here." We looked at the depression and I tried to imagine what the little building might have looked like.

Jenny then pointed to rocks piled on the right side of the hole. "That's where the chimney used to be."

I fit that piece into my mental picture. "That makes sense."

"When they mined here, the mining company thought they might bring tourists up here to the hotel. But they never finished it, and it was only used for mine workers. After they left, it was neglected and finally collapsed."

Then she gestured to a small tent nestled under the trees to the left of the hotel site, perched just above the meadow. "That's my tent."

We continued to the clearing and she pointed up at the basalt buttress towering above us. "See those white spots on the green slopes just below the rocks? Those are mountain goats. They come out almost every evening."

It didn't take us long to find the little specks that she indicated.

"I see them!" Tim excitedly. He was fascinated. I have to admit, so was I.

"If you want, tomorrow morning I'll take you up there and we'll explore a little bit," Jenny offered.

She suggested that the three of us climb up the slope below the buttress to check out the area where we had seen the goats.

"I'm not sure," Tim said hesitantly. "That looks really steep."

I looked at the climb and could see why a six-year-old might find it daunting. The map showed that the elevation gain to the basalt columns was eight hundred feet, and closely spaced contour lines emphasized the steepness. Tim had never undertaken such a challenge.

Nevertheless, I said, "Sure, that sounds like fun. You can do it, Tim."

"Great! Meet me here in the morning about nine o'clock."

"Will do," I promised.

Tim found his first backpacking dinner tasty, but his appetite may have been helped by the activity of the day. Afterward, we cleaned up and then climbed into bed for a restful sleep.

The next morning, we met up with Jenny under a cobalt-blue sky. Tim still had his doubts about the upcoming exploration.

"I'm sure you can do it," Jenny encouraged him. "We'll go slow and we won't leave you behind."

"Come on, Tim," I added. "It'll be fun."

Jenny led us over to the edge of the meadow. "We have to cross it to get to the base of the slope." She pointed over to our grassy goal.

"But we can't leave the trail," Tim said. "How are we going to get over there?"

"In some places you can walk in the grass and flowers to get where you want to go," she explained. "But there's a special way to do it. When you're in a group like we are, we spread out as we walk. Don't step in the same tracks as your friends and walk on rocks when you can. Then the plants won't be stressed so much."

Jenny took a few steps into the meadow and said to Tim, "Now you walk over there," pointing to her right. She turned to me and said, "You walk over there," pointing to her left. "And watch out for old mining stuff sticking out of the ground. It's easy to trip over."

We passed quite a few pieces of rusted metal that were sticking up several inches out of the soil. They looked like U-shaped rods whose ends had been driven into the dirt, leaving small loops showing, just big enough to catch the toe of a boot. We made our way cautiously to the bottom of the slope.

"You ready to try it, Tim?" I asked.

"I guess so."

"Then let's go!" Jenny started up the hill.

The hillside consisted of compacted dirt hummocks sparsely covered with tufts of grass. Lupine and red paint-brush made appearances here and there. On either side of us, subalpine firs marched up and down the slope in long, narrow formations. The slope was indeed steep. Steep enough in places that we had to reach out and grab rocks that jutted out or branches from scrubby bushes to make sure we gained elevation, rather than sliding back down the hill. At first, Tim stopped every three minutes or so to voice his doubts, but Jenny and I encouraged him. "Just a little bit farther!"

It took about an hour, but eventually the sum of these encouraging "little bit farther" comments brought us to our goal. The grass grew thicker up here and the top of the slope we had been climbing was treeless. The grade eased off as we reached the base of the basalt cliff. The steep basalt buttress thrust up almost vertically to meet the deep-blue sky above us. We could go no higher.

We rested on some big rocks at the base of the cliff and ate a snack. If the views from the meadow below had been awesome, we found that the panorama we now enjoyed was utterly stunning. Tim's enjoyment of the view drove all thoughts of the climb's difficulty from his mind.

The ridge opposite us sloped up toward the peak of Mount Ruth, with the top of Mount Rainier towering above its right shoulder. The ridge continued to gain elevation until it reached the point of Steamboat Prow. We could see most of Inter Glacier flowing down from the highest point of the Prow and confined by another rock barrier on the far side. Though it didn't start at the top of the mountain, this heavy load of ice and snow that moved inexorably downhill, driven by its own weight, was indeed a glacier as its name indicated.

To the right of Inter Glacier, the ridge fell to a sandy low spot called St. Elmo Pass. On the other side of the pass, the Winthrop Glacier lay hidden. The ridge continued to the right, topped by a series of broken towers that defined the west wall of the basin. This was an enhanced view of what we had seen from below, with more detail and perspective made possible by our high perch.

"Look over there at Inter Glacier." Jenny pointed. "See those little black dots? Those are climbers."

We watched the dots creep up and down the glacier. Most of these tiny specks moved in groups of three or more. Some of these rope teams moved uphill, climbers aspiring to summit the mountain. Others came down after making their attempts. I knew the climbers were buoyed by feelings of accomplishment or burdened by the disappointment of the failure to reach their goal. I looked at Tim, and his expression showed that he felt his own sense of accomplishment. He had conquered a challenge he had been sure was out of his reach.

Jenny suggested we turn around and look at a ridge with low summits behind us. "That's Second and First Burroughs, two high points on the Burroughs ridge. Sunrise is beyond them. When I'm hiking out, I work my way up the hillside over there." She pointed toward a slope above camp. "And then I hike out over Burroughs."

"Is there a trail?" I asked.

"If you go less than a mile back down the trail you hiked in on, there's another trail that takes off and heads up toward Burroughs," she said. "But I'd have to lose a lot of elevation— maybe 800 feet—and then climb back up again. It's a gain of only 1,200 feet from Glacier Basin if I just hike cross-country."

After our rest break, Jenny suggested we take time to check out the grass around us. "Maybe we can find clumps of goat hair," she said.

We spread out and soon Tim shouted, "Look!" He pointed to fuzzy white fur snagged by some of the alpine plants. "Is that it?"

"It sure is," Jenny told him.

Tim set about collecting several bunches of fur. With each fuzzy wad of hair, he grew more excited. He was actually touching goat hair, and holding it in his hand! For him, this made the whole trip worth it. The furry clumps were the early pieces of a collection that he added to several times over the years.

After we were done gathering fur, we traversed the slope as we worked our way back down. We hoped to glimpse a few of the hairy beasts that had left their calling cards, but it was the wrong time of day and they evidently spent their siestas somewhere else.

After lunch back in camp, Tim and I had plenty of time to wander up the climber's trail toward the upper basin. He loved the fuzzy-topped "mouse-on-a-stick" plants. I encouraged his interest, since my boys usually didn't care about the flowers that I found so fascinating.

This *Anemone*, known as western pasqueflower, blooms early. After their white blossoms are spent, the plant develops seedpods whose fanciful fuzzy globes could have been invented by Dr. Seuss. Their form also earns them several other descriptive names, such as "towhead baby" and "mop top." But for years, I would think of them as "Tim's flower."

Several years later, while camping at Upper Crystal Lake near the east border of the Park, I would learn that deer also love these fuzzy seedpods. One morning I woke up early and stuck my head out of my tent just in time to watch a doe wander through the meadow. I watched her move from fuzzy top to furry pod, nipping off the seeds for an early morning snack. *So that explains all the topless stems I've been seeing around here*, I'd thought.

On this first camping trip with Tim, I also discovered Cusick's speedwell, or Veronica, for the first time. I found this little wildflower enchanting, though Tim wasn't impressed. Each three- to four-inch stem has several dark-violet flowers, each with a white eye in the center. Long, delicate stamens extend from the center, with tiny yellow tips. This creates an effect of a bouquet of vibrant flowers surrounded by a cloud of yellow sparkles. On a later trip up to Camp Schurman, this hardy high-altitude bloomer would surprise and delight me when I found it among barren rocks and pumice near the top of Steamboat Prow.

Before Tim and I reached the steepest part of the primitive trail the climbers used, we turned off and made our way through the rocks down to the creek that tumbled through the valley, turbulent with meltwater from the snowfields and Inter Glacier above.

We found a way to cross the rushing water, jumping from rock to rock. Then we discovered a flat, easy path through boulder fields and sandy terrain, as we headed toward the slope on the opposite side of the valley from camp. I realized we were following the remnants of old mining roads. This made the going much easier here than in other parts of the valley floor.

Once we reached the bottom of the ridge, we found water flowing from a small opening at the base of the hillside. Rusted box-shaped objects—remnants of equipment from an old mine—and other pieces of abandoned machinery lay clustered around the opening. We felt like explorers discovering treasure as we found these artifacts in the Park. Water-loving flowers, including yellow monkey-flowers, thrived in the marshy, mossy ground that bordered a trickle of water flowing from the old mine entrance. We had no clear concept of how the early history of the area influenced the basin. *It's a national park. It should be pristine. Right?*

We made our way back across the valley to our tent site. As we sat on one of the logs, I asked Tim, "Did you have a good time today?"

"Yeah, I did. I really liked finding that goat hair!"

"The mining stuff was interesting, too, wasn't it?"

"Yeah, I guess," he said distractedly as he checked his pockets for his fur collection.

Contentment filled me as I looked at my little explorer.

Our second night in the tent started much the same as the first, quiet and cozy. But soon after we dropped off to sleep, the clang of metal suddenly jolted us awake.

"What's that?" Tim asked, alarmed.

"I don't know," I whispered into the darkness. Visions of bears went through my head.

Tim's, too. "Is it a bear?" he asked.

"I don't think so," I said to reassure him. Though I didn't really know.

It took me several seconds to place the sound. "I think our pot and stove might have been knocked over," I said. I had left them just a couple of feet in front of our tent door, the pot sitting on the stove, both of them perched on a rock. Suddenly, that didn't feel far enough away.

We lay in the darkness, listening to the silence outside. No snuffling, grunting, or any other animal sounds. After a couple of minutes, I decided to check on our surroundings. "You stay here while I see what's going on," I told Tim. He didn't argue.

I tentatively opened the tent door and stuck my head out. My flashlight illuminated the scene—the pot rested on its side next to the stove on the ground. Then I shone the flashlight on our food bag, which dangled from a tree limb just a couple of feet above the stove. We'd noticed rodents around our camp earlier, but I hadn't considered the possibility of other beasts. The bag still hung in its place, now spinning around in lazy rotation. I slipped on my shoes, quietly made my way out of the tent, and looked more closely. Something shiny and wet clung to the sides of the bag.

An examination of the soft dirt near the tent door and the stove yielded good clues. I saw a clear imprint of a hoof, and then another. Deer tracks. Evidently, a deer had been looking for something in our camp—perhaps salt—and thought she could get it by licking our food bag. *Whew!*

"It's not a bear," I said softly to Tim through the tent wall. "It was just a deer. Nothing to worry about."

I repositioned the food bag, hanging it much higher to remove the temptation from the deer. I set the pot and stove nearer the tent, and refrained from stacking them. As I crawled back into the tent and squirmed into my sleeping bag, I reassured Tim that everything was fine. It took us a little while, but eventually we fell back asleep.

In the years before and after this trip, I have been warned about mice, chipmunks, and bears going after food, but never about thieving deer.

When we emerged from our tent the next morning, we saw that the great weather was holding. We found the hike out easier than the hike in. Of course. It was downhill. And we no longer had a sense of the unknown. We rested in the dark forest near the midway point, which Jenny had told us was col-loquially called "Sherwood Forest," before continuing on. We had made a new friend, and would spend more time with her over the next few years.

When we reached our red-and-white GMC Jimmy in the parking lot and changed out of our hiking boots, the experi-ence was complete. Tim had discovered he could do things he had never imagined and that exploring the outdoors could be fun. He had conquered a mountain—the first of many—and his stash of goat hair was a tangible reminder of the adventure.

We had no idea how many great adventures still lay ahead of us.

THE WINDS OF CAMP SCHURMAN

Deep down inside me a tiny voice was calling.
At first scarcely audible, it persisted until I
could no longer ignore it. It was the voice of
the wild places, and I knew that it was now
part of me forever. Inexplicably—amazingly—I
knew I loved that hell. Its fiendish grasp had
captured me, and I wanted to see it again.

—Percy Fawcett, Amazon explorer
who disappeared in 1925

When can I climb Mount Rainier again? When can I actually step on the very top? After my first summit attempt with Bob and Ken in June 1988, this refrain played constantly in my thoughts, an undercurrent to everything I did. I avoided thinking about the ferocious gale we'd experienced our second night.

I had yet to go back. After I'd taken the boys for a couple of overnight trips after the adventure with Ken and Bob, Larry and I had discussed the possibility of me looking for work. Tim would be starting kindergarten in the fall, providing me with some free time. A new REI store—filled with all kinds of outdoor gear for adventure junkies—had opened earlier in the summer not more than fifteen minutes from our house. After my recent experiences with hiking and climbing, this seemed like the ideal place to apply. I liked that I could work part-time, mostly while the kids were in school or in the evenings after Larry came home from work.

I applied in early August. When I dropped off the application, I was met by the assistant manager, Laura Valle, a vivacious dark-haired woman who barely reached my height of five foot three. She gave me a catalog of the products they offered, which I diligently studied to prepare for my interview.

Within a week, I was called in for an interview. I met with Brian, the tall, spare manager, who led me to a couple of chairs in a quiet corner of the shoe department. I answered all his questions, impressing him with my knowledge of tents, sleeping bags, types of insulation, and other camping gear. He offered me a job before I even left the meeting.

"When do you want me to start?" I asked.

"Next week, if you can," he replied quickly. "We need someone in our camping department, where we sell sleeping bags and tents."

I agreed, and my name appeared on the work schedule a few days before Labor Day weekend.

When I showed up on my first day, I learned that my department sold a few other categories of camping gear besides those Brian had mentioned, including water bottles, stoves, socks, and jackets. We were also responsible for the rental department, where customers could check out hiking and climbing gear.

I quickly caught up on the information I needed to become a good sales associate. The reason behind the store's urgent need for another staff member quickly became apparent. Several coworkers planned to head to Mount Rainier on Labor Day weekend to make a summit attempt, leaving a skeleton staff to cover the store.

This filled me with envy. *I really want to climb again! My conditioning is as good as it has ever been.* After my climb with Ken and Bob, and after dozens of hikes during the spring and summer, I felt strong. My two overnights with the boys, to Glacier Basin with Tim and to Mystic Lake with Kris, were the icing on the cake. These factors offset any hesitation I felt whenever I remembered the winds that Ken, Bob, and I had experienced near the summit and at night when gusts of wind had pushed a tent wall into our faces. I felt ready to go!

It was not to be. I watched with longing and kept my mouth shut as my coworkers prepared. Soon they crowded into several vehicles and headed for the mountain. I fulfilled my responsibilities. I showed up to my new job and just imagined what it would be like to return to the land of glaciers and rocks.

Three days later the group returned.

"How'd it go?" I asked the first person I saw.

"We didn't make it past Camp Muir," came the answer, full of disappointment. "Too many people in the group weren't prepared for how hard it was."

This answer helped offset the regrets I felt. I remembered the difficulty of the climb. It came as no surprise that some had been forced to turn back.

The experience of working in the store, though, opened me up to a whole new set of possibilities. I found myself in the midst of a group of coworkers who shared my interests. They hiked, they climbed, they skied, they rode bikes. They enjoyed all of these activities and more.

Before long, a great idea came to me. At least I thought it was great. *I'll talk to my new coworkers and find some who want to make another attempt on the mountain. We can plan to climb next summer, in June. And we'll try the other side of Mount Rainier, the side Ken told me about.*

During our trip together, Ken had said to me, "I've always wanted to climb the route on the northeast side that goes through Camp Schurman, but I've never had the chance."

"Is that side harder than going through Camp Muir?" I'd wanted to know.

"Not really," he said. "It's just different. You follow a trail through trees for three miles until you get to Glacier Basin where there's a big green meadow. Then you hike on a trail through rocks until you reach Inter Glacier. From there it's all uphill to the camp."

It sounded like a much more interesting approach compared to slogging up snowfields to Camp Muir.

I'd had Ken's description of this route in mind when I chose Glacier Basin as the destination for Tim's first backpacking trip. We'd completed that camping trip two months before I started my job. While exploring with Tim, I'd become familiar with the first part of the Camp Schurman route. If my coworkers and I organized this climb, I figured I could invite Ken to come along and he could realize his dream.

Over the course of the winter, a small group of fellow employees committed to the adventure. These included Ken Blue, an energetic, dark-haired assistant manager in his thirties, whose lean body of average height didn't scream "climber" to me. I learned, however, that he had gained plenty of climbing experience in Alaska. This included work as a rescue ranger on Denali, formerly known as Mount McKinley.

The second experienced climber in the group worked in the same department I did. At nearly six feet, Mike Brown stood a little taller than Ken B. His sandy-brown hair was thinning, and a few gray hairs were sprinkled in his beard and mustache. A quiet man, Mike didn't brag about his experience. But at forty-something years old, he'd spent a lot of time outdoors, both during summer and winter. Besides being a seasoned climber, he was an expert telemark skier.

Paul Robson was the youngest of the group. He had not yet reached his twentieth birthday. But this five-foot, ten-inch tall young man had already experienced a harrowing ordeal on Mount Rainier when he was seventeen.

He had been climbing with his father and several friends when one of the men broke through a snowbridge and fell into a crevasse. When he fell, a large quantity of the snow from the snowbridge had also fallen in and solidified around him. Paul was the only person in the party who was small enough to be lowered down to the man in the confines of the crevasse. The climbing team had lowered him into the gaping hole to try to dig the man out. Unfortunately, the fallen snow had set like concrete, and Paul didn't have the tools or enough time to dig through it to free him. Paul had watched as the man slowly succumbed to his injuries and the freezing temperatures of his tomb. Even with this experience, though, Paul said he wanted to accompany the rest of us.

Another coworker, Rick, also threw his hat in the ring. He eagerly agreed to try anything his idol, Ken B., took part in. Not much older than Paul, Rick wore his dark hair longer than the rest of the guys, almost down to his collar. His build was similar to Ken B.'s, though he was a bit thinner and a tad shorter.

Though Rick worked in the store with us, his ultimate goal was to become a police officer. He had the least climbing experience of anyone in the group—only one trip to Camp Muir under his belt. He declared his willingness to get in shape, though, and Ken B. promised to teach him what he needed to know about crampons, ice axes, and self-arrest.

In the midst of our planning, I contacted Ken Smith.

"How would you like to go on another climb?" I asked him over the phone. "We plan to go through Camp Schurman, and you'll get your chance to tackle that side."

I could hear the enthusiasm in his voice when he said, "Sure. Just let me know the details."

The expedition now included three climbers with extensive experience—Ken S., Ken B., and Mike. They would share the duties of leaders, while I worked on logistics. None of us had been on this route before. The stage was set.

We set off on a Monday in June 1989, determined to avoid the crowds that ascended to Camp Schurman on the weekends. We noticed a few clouds floating slowly through an azure sky while walking through the forest to Glacier Basin, but weather reports had been optimistic and we enjoyed the warmth of the plentiful sunshine. The weather continued to cooperate as we worked our way up Inter Glacier to a high, snow-free ridge. Then we dropped down to the Emmons Glacier.

We roped up before stepping onto the Emmons, our group splitting into two teams of three. Then we headed up toward Camp Schurman. We worked our way up the snowy glacier, stepping across small crevasses that stretched across the slope.

A small stone hut gave away the location of the camp above. At an elevation of 9,460 feet, it sits on bare rock where Steamboat Prow divides the Emmons and Winthrop Glaciers. Our plodding pace slowly brought us to the saddle. Upon arrival, we looked around the rocky spit that stretched out from Steamboat Prow, which towered above us. For the first time, I had the opportunity to look at the hut at Camp Schurman, where the rangers stayed when they patrolled the area. The solid structure stood at the base of the Prow, serving as an enduring monument to adventure.

A coworker had told me how a group of climbers, members of the outdoor club called The Mountaineers, had erected the hut between 1958 and 1961 to serve as a shelter during inclement weather. She was a member of the club and was proud of their accomplishment.

Eventually, the Park Service took over and transformed it into a home away from home for climbing rangers. These rangers had specialized duties and provided an added layer of safety to climbers who ascended the mountain, keeping an eye on the throngs who traveled on Mount Rainier's icy glaciers.

When describing the hut, I now tell people to picture a very large corrugated culvert with about a third of it cut off at the point where the sides meet the ground. The builders who made it cemented rocks all over the corrugated metal surface and built wooden walls on each end. The back end displays one small window, looking out on the sheer cliff rising to the top of Steamboat Prow. The other end, broken up by a window and a door, faces the bulk of Mount Rainier, which towers another 4,900 feet higher. The view of the Emmons and Winthrop Glaciers flowing down from the summit adds to the grandeur. Stone benches run along the length of the hut on each side.

We checked out the hut and found a secure latch on the door. A man clad in a down jacket and insulated pants stood next to a nearby tent and noticed us investigating it.

"The rangers aren't here," he offered. "They don't come up on Mondays or Tuesdays."

We acknowledged this information and shifted our attention to the snow-free saddle.

Mike and the two Kens took stock of the tent sites on the sandy surface of the saddle. Most of them were already occupied. Then they saw three or four other tents set up in the snow on the edge of the Winthrop Glacier. The colorful tents included one with bright-blue and yellow triangles sewn together into a rounded shape and a dark-yellow tent shaped like a dome.

They conferred and then Ken B. turned to the rest of us. "Let's go over there." He pointed toward the tents on the

Winthrop. "We'll pitch our tents directly on the snow. You all have good sleeping pads, right?"

We nodded in agreement.

By using ice axes and snow shovels to create flat areas, and then walking around to tamp down the snow, we could easily create tent platforms right on the glacier.

Before doing anything else, I dropped my pack and helped Ken carve out our tent site. Then I looked around for the outhouse. I spotted it about fifty feet down the Winthrop, just off a steep wall of rocks rising up to Steamboat Prow. The old wooden structure sat in the snow and leaned slightly to the side. Its bleached boards showed the effects of sun and scouring wind.

I approached the tiny building and looked for the door, finding it on the downhill side that faced away from the camping area. Its latched was closed, so I thought someone must be inside. However, I could hear no noise or see no sign of movement.

After almost a minute, I called out, "Is anybody in there?"

I heard no response and tentatively opened the latch. An empty space greeted me. I stepped in and found little snowdrifts in the corners. Surprisingly, I didn't need to hold my breath. This early in the season, with cold temperatures still holding a grip on the camp, the place gave off a negligible amount of the typical noxious outhouse smell.

Once inside, I saw a handwritten sign posted on the back of the door that stated, "Please latch the door when you leave so it won't get damaged by the wind."

I learned that occupants usually left the door open to enjoy the view below, which stretched all the way to Puget Sound. When a new person approached, they were expected to stick their head around the corner just far enough to see if the door stood open. A closed door meant it was safe to go in.

When I arrived back in camp, it was time to set up the tent. Ken S. and I shared a little green Early Winters tube tent that I'd acquired through connections at REI. Though it was used, the tent was in great condition and provided just the right amount of space for two people to spread out their pads and sleeping bags in cozy proximity. Two fiberglass tent poles bent to form arches, a small one at the feet and a larger arch at the shoulders. These lifted the tent walls away from its occupants.

Unlike the camping tent that Ken, Bob, and I had shared on my first Mount Rainier climb, this tent was designed to take on severe weather. Once the tent was staked out at each end and along the sides, the low profile of its tube shape was supposed to stand up well to the high winds people often encountered at high elevations.

The manufacturer had used a unique fabric when constructing the tent—GORE-TEX. A recent innovation at the time, this breathable, waterproof fabric was used primarily to make rain gear. Using it to make a tent had taken the concept one step further. The fabric provided a big advantage for the climber—it cut down on weight. Unlike the usual double-walled tents that used a body and a rainfly to deal with condensation, a GORE-TEX tent required only a single layer of protection. This had allowed Ken and me to save a couple of pounds of weight in our packs. And every ounce counted.

Paul had planned a different approach. He intended to sleep in a bivouac sack—climbers call it a *bivy* sack—in the snow. The bright-red bag with its blue stripes down each side used GORE-TEX, just like my tent, making it waterproof. It was just a little over six feet long and almost three feet wide. Using no poles, it was just big enough to accommodate Paul's insulated pad on the bottom with his sleeping bag on top. He planned to crawl inside at bedtime and close up everything snug around his head. The waterproof, breathable characteristics of the fabric were intended to prevent condensation on the inside of the sack, even when it was completely closed.

Ken and I watched him dig a trench about six feet long and two feet deep in the snow near our door.

"Are you going to sleep in a hole?" I asked.

"This should protect me from the wind," he told me.

"Good thing you're close by," Ken said. "We can keep an eye on you that way."

"I don't think I'll need it." Paul delivered this comment with a smirk.

Mike, Rick, and Ken B. shared a tent that they erected about twenty feet up the glacier from our site. The new REI-designed tent—made of vivid yellow, red, and purple material—was borrowed from our store's rental department. It also included features designed to deal with the double-wall issue. Though this tent was made with only one layer, its fabric didn't breathe. The walls draped down from a single ridgepole that was supported by two more poles. The sidewalls extended below a waterproof "tub" formed by a panel of nylon that was sewn all the way around the floor. A strip of mesh connected the main wall to the tub. The designers had envisioned that condensation would travel down the tent wall and drip outside the tent. The mesh panel was intended to provide ventilation, to cut down on condensation.

A few weeks before, several of us had attended a company workshop where new products were highlighted. We had seen a photo of this tent set up on a patch of snow. Anxious to try out the tent, Ken B. had brought it along.

After we set up our sleeping accommodations, we focused on food preparation. As we fixed our dinners and filled our water bottles, a blanket of gray clouds rolled in and drove the sun away. The cloud cover dropped lower and lower until the mountain above us disappeared into a pearly gray nothingness. Snow started drifting down around us as we cleaned up after dinner. Before daylight fled entirely, we crawled into our sleeping bags, planning to start at one in the morning.

As I fell into a fitful sleep, I had no idea that the whispers of the snow we'd seen were only a quiet warning of what we would face over the next eighteen hours.

Not more than two hours later, the sound of voices near the tent woke me up. "We have to get this snow off of here."

I rolled over and brushed against the ceiling. Raising my hand, I discovered the ceiling only a few inches above my nose. I reached for my headlamp and turned it on. Accumulated snow weighed the fabric down, causing it to sag the full length of our tent.

Ken woke as I reached up and thrust at the fabric, knocking the snow off. He helped clear it off the tent, using his feet at the lower end. We realized we hadn't pulled the ends of the tent taut enough to keep it from sagging. An ice axe anchored the foot of the tent, and just a couple of tent stakes buried in the snow secured the head.

Neither of us wanted to get out and try to fix it. We just kept knocking off the snow every so often.

Then another thought hit us.

"How do you think Paul's doing out there?" I asked.

"I was wondering the same thing," Ken admitted.

I zipped the tent door open and stuck out my head. "Paul, are you okay?" I called.

I heard a muffled answer. "Yeah, I'm fine."

"Are you warm enough?"

"It's great in here," he replied.

I dozed off again, waking up a couple of times before midnight to knock off more snow. Long before our scheduled wake-up time arrived, it became obvious that the bad weather would prevent us from making a summit attempt. After conferring through tent walls, our group decided to roll over and go back to sleep.

When I woke again around midnight, I could feel that something had changed. A soughing wind caressed the tent, rising to a sigh and then falling into silence, as if the mountain were breathing. As the breeze passed over the tent, the walls rustled quietly, restless at its touch. I knocked snow off the tent once again and turned over to doze a bit more.

Sleep didn't last long this time. The rattle and slaps of tent walls being buffeted by gusty winds punctuated the darkness. The roof no longer sagged with snow—the wind took care of that. I listened with trepidation as the wind strengthened, howling over the saddle from the Emmons Glacier and then subsiding to a steady rush. Before long the mountain roared with each exhale, shouting with the same voice as the surf when driven by the incoming tide, though the tempo of the mountain exhalations was slower than a wave song.

The blasts of wind found the weakness of our tent setup. I soon learned that each time I heard the sound rising, a wall of wind would subsequently throw itself at the tent. The wind attacked from the side where I lay. The tent was still staked only at the head and foot. The gale continued to strengthen, the sound rising to a roar like a freight train bearing down on us.

During one particularly strong gust, the wall pushed against my shoulder and the floor rose up, the tent threatening to roll down the glacier. By then I was leaning into each blast, putting as much weight as I could into the corner at the base of the pole beside my elbow, to keep it from lifting.

Ken too had given up on sleep. Once the wind felt vicious enough to blow the tent down the glacier with us inside, he decided to go outside and reinforce our anchors. He crawled out of his sleeping bag and pulled on enough layers to protect himself during the short time he would spend facing the gale.

He stuck his head out the tent door and took a look at Paul's trench a few feet away. Drifted snow filled it, covering Paul's bivy bag. The snow appeared to be several inches deep.

Ken slipped his feet into his boots and stood up, leaning against the wind. He shouted to Paul, trying to be heard over the gale. The snow in the trench stirred and Paul sat up, still wrapped in his bivy sack. He opened the top far enough to let Ken know he was okay.

"But it feels like I'm about to smother," he shouted. "I'm going to check out the hut and see if I can get out of the wind in there."

"Isn't the hut locked?" Ken asked.

A bearded man in a red puffy jacket was walking by our tent, headed for the outhouse, and heard the question. "There are already some people inside," he said. "I don't know how they got in, but the door is unlocked."

"Sounds like a good idea, then!" Ken yelled to Paul. As Ken headed back to the tent, Paul worked his way out of his bag and trench. He gathered up his gear and headed for the hut, bent over against the gale.

Our equipment included an aluminum stake about two feet long that Ken had carried up to camp. Including this item in our gear gave us an extra layer of safety. It could be driven into the snow and used as an anchor if we needed to rescue anyone who fell into a crevasse.

The afternoon before, Ken had used it to anchor the foot of our tent, pounding it about ten inches into the snow with an ice axe. Now, he checked this stake first. It still seemed secure. But he took the time to pull the tent taut and drive the anchor in several more inches.

Stopping to brace himself during the strongest wind gusts, he made his way around the tent, driving the shafts of our ice axes into the snow at strategic points, using them to anchor the sides. Once he'd come around to my side and secured the corner of the tent where I'd wedged my elbow, my concern eased a little.

Soon he unzipped the door and came back in the tent in a flurry of snow. He crawled into his sleeping bag, but we both knew we wouldn't get much sleep before it grew light.

We lay listening to the moaning and roaring of the wind. The sound reminded me of an ebbing and flowing roar I'd once experienced while camping by the ocean. The wind now mimicked the sound of waves coming up the beach and then receding. But this powerful roar of the wind was much louder than the sound of crashing waves had been. The cadence of mountain breaths grew louder, slower, more purposeful.

During lulls in the rush, I heard voices coming from the other tents. Other climbers crawled out to check the surroundings and the security of their anchors.

After a bit, we saw the glow of a headlamp approaching through the wall of our tent. Someone leaned down near our door. We heard Ken B. shouting.

"We're going inside the hut," he told us. "Our tent is filling up with snow and it's being blown over. The poles are bent so much that it's almost flat." So much for the new design. "Those mesh panels at the bottom of the walls keep letting spindrift in, and we're lying in snowdrifts."

The wind could blow spindrift—tiny snow crystals carried by the wind—through the tiniest holes. Evidently, the pole configuration hadn't been able to stand up to these winds either. Despite the pictures we had seen of the tent set up on snow, it was actually designed for backpacking, and was not intended to be used in the elements one encountered while climbing.

Ken and I continued to listen to the wind as the darkness gave way to dim grayness, and then full cloud-covered daylight. When matters became urgent, I crawled out of my sleeping bag and prepared to head to the outhouse. After pulling warm pants over my long underwear and slipping into two jackets, I crawled quickly out the door.

Before heading down the glacier, I looked around, hoping our cook pot hadn't blown away. An unbroken blanket of powder greeted me. A little digging around revealed the pot under about four inches of snow, along with our stove.

As I stood and surveyed the nearby glacier, I realized the snow had ceased falling. The wind, however, hadn't abated one iota. If anything, it had gained strength. Clouds still obscured the mountain above, but the scene around the camp was clear.

I could see that only one or two other tents remained on the snow of the Winthrop. The dirt spit had been emptied of color. Everyone must have either taken shelter or headed down the mountain. *At least*, I thought, *my tent stood up to its billing as a good tent to use in the wind. When properly anchored.*

As I approached the outhouse, I peeked carefully around the corner for a look at the door. Closed. With a mittened hand, I pulled the cord to unlatch it. The door swung open, yanked by the wind. I gasped. A tall young man stood there, wearing a green climbing jacket and insulated pants, a gray knit cap on his head. He faced me and I sputtered, "I'm sorry! I'm sorry! The door was closed and I thought no one was in here!"

"It's okay! It's okay!" he rushed to say. "I just wanted to find a place out of the wind where I could brush my teeth."

Then I noticed the toothbrush in his hand. "I'm sorry!" I repeated.

"That's okay. I'm done," he reassured me. He stepped out of the open door and headed up the glacier toward camp.

A chuckle bubbled up in my chest. But once he was gone, I too fastened the door snug against the howling wind. The snowdrifts in the corners were twice as big as they had been the evening before. I listened carefully for footsteps so I could warn anyone who might approach that I was using the place. Thankfully, nobody interrupted.

I worked my way back to the tent where Ken S. was standing outside. "Let's go inside the hut with everybody else," he suggested. "We don't really need to keep fighting this."

I looked at my little green tent. I was proud of how it had performed in the wind. It had done its job, mocking the wind with its sturdiness, even if at times the fiberglass poles had bent at alarming angles. But I, too, felt beaten down by the howling, buffeting threat and roaring noise of the maelstrom. We quickly took the tent down, gripping it tightly as we folded it, the gale nearly tearing it out of our hands. We gathered the rest of our gear and moved all of it up to a stone bench on the leeward side of the hut.

The wind howled and pushed at us like a giant hand as we cautiously made our way around the corner of the hut to the wooden door. We hung on with a firm grip when we opened it and stepped inside, escaping the unrelenting blast.

Once the door was securely closed, I took in the small room, tall enough and big enough to have a set of two bunks on each side. The high ceiling allowed the inhabitants to stand up straight with extra room. A short ladder attached to the left wall led up to a trapdoor, evidently there to allow access to the space above the ceiling. A substantial lock on the door kept pilferers out. At the far end of the room, cupboards for cooking gear and food lined the walls above a counter. A small gas stove stood on a platform under the back window.

Bodies crowded the open space. A few people sat in the bunks against the walls, and the rest stood. The humid air smelled like sweaty clothes, sunscreen, and stove fuel. Body heat warmed the hut, so I shed my jacket. Even with the wind howling outside, two layers of long underwear and fleece kept me warm.

Spying an empty upper bunk in the far left corner, I made my way through the crowd of mostly men. I crawled up into the bunk, a rectangle of canvas laced to a metal frame, and listened to the chatter around me.

"Did you see the wind gauge? It said one or two gusts were over a hundred miles per hour!" A man near the front door pointed at an instrument in a cupboard to the left of the door.

Next to the anemometer I saw a radio. Another climber, tall with dark hair sticking out every direction, saw it, too. He asked, "Has anybody called the ranger station?"

All he got were shrugs and a murmured "no" from a nearby individual. The dark-haired man turned away, evidently not wanting to be the first to try to call the ranger station at White River.

The door opened again and a man in a bright-chartreuse jacket squeezed into the hut with two other men, letting in a blast of cold air. He looked around at the crowded place. "Wow! This place is packed!"

A short man with blond hair wearing a blue jacket spoke up. "That damn wind tore up my tent."

The chartreuse-clad man responded, "It blew my sleeping bag into a crevasse down below us!"

From the back, I heard, "Our tent got blown away, too. Who knows where it ended up!"

I tried to figure out how many people were taking shelter in this small hut. They took up all of the sitting, lying, and standing space available. After counting twice, sixteen seemed to be a safe guess.

After an hour or so, I decided it would be a good idea to have snacks nearby, especially if we were going to be holed up for a while. I dropped over the edge of the bunk and squeezed my way through the crowd. Listening for a lull in the wind, I opened the door when it seemed like the howling had ebbed somewhat. Even at the wind's lowest point, though, I needed to hang on tightly to keep the door from banging against the outer wall.

Bracing against the force of the wind at my back, I crept along the wall to the corner. I turned into the lee of the hut and found myself in a transformed world. Though the wind still swirled here, the rock-solid hut had robbed it of its power.

I found my pack and dug out my food bag. Then I headed back to the corner of the hut so I could creep to the door. I listened for a lull. When it seemed the howl had abated slightly, I stepped out of the sheltered haven. With my first step forward, a vicious gust hit the saddle from my left. In my peripheral vision, a couple of feet to the right, I saw where the ground dropped off six feet to a jumble of rocks below. Instinct kicked in and I fell flat to the ground.

The roar of the wind sounded like a tornado passing over me. After several seconds it subsided to a persistent rushing noise. I pushed myself to my knees. Shaking with adrenaline, I rose to a crouch and crept over to the door. The wind stole my breath and I had to gasp for air until I found myself inside the hut with the door closed again.

The upper bunk in the back remained empty, so I made my way back to my retreat. Ken S. stood near the stove. "What do you think?" I asked him. "How long are we going stay here?"

"It doesn't hurt to wait it out," he replied. "There's no reason to hurry down. Nobody's expecting us to come home until tomorrow."

I scrambled into my bunk and checked to see what remained in my food bag. As I munched on a granola bar, I listened to the chatter around me.

Soon, a quiet voice said, "Does it seem like it's dying down?"

"Maybe, just a little bit," someone said.

"I think we should try it," said a firm voice. "We can't stay here forever." Three men moved toward the front of the hut, their carabiners jingling.

Over the next hour, groups of two, three, and four people gathered their gear, put on their harnesses, prepared their ropes, and headed out the door. By ten in the morning, only two people remained besides our group.

Ken S., Mike, and Ken B. put their heads together and decided that instead of trying to wait for the storm to blow over, we would attempt to descend.

"I think the wind has died down a little," Ken B. said. It didn't seem that way to me, but they were our leaders.

"I don't think we should rope up," Mike said. "That would be just one more thing we'd have to deal with."

Ken S. shrugged. Ken B. said, "Sounds good to me."

We left the safety of the hut and braced ourselves, leaning into the force that threatened to shove us off the spit. Cautiously, we moved along the wall and rounded the corner of the hut into the lee side of the structure, where our packs waited on the stone bench. I took it as a good sign when I didn't get blown over the drop-off along the way.

While we arranged the gear in our packs, Rick pointed toward the trail. "Look," he said. "Those last two guys are taking off." I paused to watch them fight the gusts as they moved away from the hut.

We finished loading up and headed toward the trail in the snow where the descent to the glacier began.

The wind's ebb and flow continued as we huddled together at the top of the trail before starting down. When it howled the hardest and threatened to blow us away like pieces of chaff, we faced into it and hunched over, bracing ourselves with our ice axes thrust into the snow.

"Just move when it calms down." Mike's soft voice almost disappeared in the rushing wind.

"You lead," Ken B. told him.

Mike started down the trail and we followed at intervals of about twenty feet. A cliff of ice with a small cornice curling toward us loomed on our right, at the top of the trail. An intimidating crevasse defined the edge of the trail below us on our left. I ended up fourth in line, with Paul ahead of me and Rick following. Our group moved in fits and starts down the glacier. Whenever we heard the wind gather itself and start to howl up the glacier, we bent over our ice axes and braced ourselves. Once it had temporarily spent itself, we rushed twenty or thirty steps ahead, stopping when we heard the next wave coming.

The route off the Emmons Glacier followed a small trail through rocks and over loose dirt, angling up the ridge between Inter Glacier and the Emmons. One by one, we reached the edge of the glacier and started up the trail. Below us, a huge crevasse yawned between the icy glacier and jagged rocks exposed at the bottom of the ridge.

The wind grew stronger with each step, as if trying to prevent our escape. The gusts like inhalations ceased, and the wind remained a steady exhale, its current pushing against my body and threatening to use my pack as a sail to blow me away. I lowered myself to my knees and shuffled along, using my ice axe as an anchor. Plant the axe—shuffle—shuffle—then move the ice axe again. Paul, ahead of me, used a similar technique.

The howling gale grew even stronger. I sat down and pulled myself along the little trail of crusty snow, my butt sliding along the frozen footsteps of previous climbers, my body still anchored by my ice axe.

Looking ahead every so often, I saw the slope of the trail finally ease off, then disappear around the shoulder of the ridge above us. Several feet later, I decided the wind had abated enough to allow me to get back up on my knees. I rolled off my bottom, my big pack heavy on my back. I picked up my ice axe to drive the shaft into the next anchor spot. *Whoosh!* The hand of the furies knocked me sideways and started me rolling down the snowy slope.

The thought of the gaping crevasse below, where the glacier met the side of the ridge, flashed through my mind. *I've got to stop myself!* I thought. *Self-arrest! Self-arrest!*

After tumbling head over heels, I managed to roll to my stomach and maneuver my feet downhill. I tried to dig the pick of my ice axe into the snow, but the wind-scoured surface, hard as icy cement, resisted. Still, I dragged it along, getting just enough traction to slow my slide. The thought of digging my toes in scared me. I knew that if the prongs of my crampons bit into the snow before my body slowed down, I could flip over.

My body's friction, the pick of the ice axe in my right hand, and my mittened left hand digging into the snow were enough to stop my descent. When I realized I had come to a stop, I said a frantic, silent prayer.

Can they bring in a helicopter for me? If I get off this mountain, I'll never come back! I opened my eyes and saw only dim gray light. My sunglasses had filled with snow as I slid, and my vision was completely obscured.

Only a few seconds passed before I heard voice shouting, "Are you okay? Are you okay?"

Rick scrabbled carefully down the hard, snowy slope until he could reach a strap on the top of my pack. As he grabbed it, he asked again, "Judy, are you all right?"

The weight of my pack eased a little, reassuring me. I took a deep breath and said weakly, "I'm okay. I just can't see."

I carefully eased my sunglasses off my face and ran a mittened thumb around the inside of the lenses before putting them back on. Now only water drops made it hard to see. After a few deep breaths, I looked around and evaluated my situation. We had actually made it around the crest of the ridge. When the wind had blown me over, I'd rolled straight down the ridge, away from the crevasse below.

Paul moved carefully down beside Rick. "Can you move?" he shouted. "Everybody's waiting for us just around the corner. The wind isn't so bad there."

"I guess so." I got to my hands and knees and slowly crawled back up to the beaten trail. Rick kept a hand on my pack.

We found the rest of our team sitting just ten or fifteen feet farther down the trail. The curve up the slope offered some shelter, and the wind had eased off so there was less danger of being blown away.

We took a water and snack break while I caught my breath. Then we headed down the glacier. Adrenaline fueled my descent to Glacier Basin.

As we paused at the bottom of Inter Glacier, we saw a lone figure below us making his way slowly up the trail. As he drew close, I saw he was a young man, clad in a warm jacket and water-resistant pants, his head protected by a wool cap.

"Hi." He lifted his hand.

"Hi," Ken S. answered. "You're going the wrong way."

The smiling man stopped when he got closer. "I'm a ranger," he told us. "They sent me up here to check on everyone."

"We were the last climbers to leave the hut," Mike said. "Everyone else already went down."

"That's good to know," the ranger said. "It means I don't have to go up there."

"You really don't want to fight your way up there on your own." Ken B. gestured to me. "Judy here almost got blown into a crevasse!"

"Really? Are you all right?"

"Yeah, I'm okay. I was on my knees, and the wind *still* blew me over."

"I can believe it," the ranger said. "I talked to a group who camped near the Japanese Gardens, down there above the yellow hill." He pointed to a green spot near some old mine tailings on the opposite slope. "Even there, where it's more sheltered, the wind was strong enough to destroy one of their tents."

"This is unbelievable!" Paul said.

"Thanks for the information," the ranger said. "I'll go a little farther, but it sounds like everyone made it out."

The rest of our slog down the trail and through the forest passed in a blur.

When we reached the trailhead, I faced a quandary. We had planned for Larry to come pick me up the next day. I hitched a ride to the ranger station where we signed out and tried to call him on a pay phone. No answer. Mike offered to give me a ride, which solved the problem.

When we checked in with the ranger, he told us, "We've heard reports that six or seven tents were lost or destroyed up at Camp Schurman," the ranger said, "and even one all the way down in Glacier Basin." The wind offered no mercy.

Mike drove me to my house. Sure enough, Larry's car was missing from the driveway. He had taken the boys somewhere. Tired and hungry, my priorities were food first and a shower second. I craved a big steak, salty potato chips, and a glass of wine, but my wallet, including my driver's license, was still in Larry's car. I took some money from our spare cash stash, grabbed my car keys, and headed to a nearby store.

At the checkout counter, the clerk glanced at me as she passed the wine over the scanner. "Can I see some ID, please?" There it was again—the problem of looking so much younger than my age.

I looked at her and lost it. "I've just come down from climbing Mount Rainier where I almost got blown down the mountain. I'm tired and hungry! I'm thirty-six years old, and my husband has my ID! I just want to take my stuff and go home and eat and take a shower!"

She looked at me with wide eyes. The face of the man in line behind me showed a similar expression. Then she sputtered, "That's okay, that's okay."

She put the wine in the bag with the other items and rang up the purchase. Neither of us said anything as I handed her my cash and she gave me change. Her gaze followed me as I headed out the door.

The dinner and shower were heavenly.

Immediately following my self-arrest on Inter Glacier, I had impulsively vowed never to come back. But my promise to stay off the mountain didn't last long. Within weeks, I found myself regretting the missed opportunity to make it to the top. I started planning how I might try again.

Fourteen more attempts up the slopes of Mount Rainier, several of them successful, would follow in subsequent years.

Close your eyes and turn your face into the wind.
Feel it sweep along your skin in an
invisible ocean of exultation.
Suddenly, you *know* you are *alive*.

—Vera Nazarian

GOATS FOR
NEIGHBORS

The Lord God is my strength,
He makes my feet like the feet of a deer,
He enables me to tread on the heights.

—Habakkuk 3:19

My success on Mount Rainier the previous summer and our recent aborted attempt in June had given me confidence in my ability to handle a big pack. The success of my three-day hikes with each of the boys had inspired a decision to take them on a two-night trip together. Tim still had taken only one backpacking trip, to Glacier Basin. Kris had gone on his second outing, to Mystic Lake on the north side of Mount Rainier, soon after Tim's hike. Each of the boys had grown a couple of inches in the last year. By then, in 1989, they were ready to carry a little more gear.

I'd chosen Summerland in Mount Rainier National Park as our destination because I'd seen its flower-strewn meadows and gorgeous views on a previous day hike. The four-and-a-half-mile hike to Summerland added only a mile to the distance that Tim had walked on his first backpacking trip. I thought the kids could handle that, along with the 2,000-feet elevation gain. Kris's trip to Mystic Lake had been a grueling seven miles each way, three miles more than his first hike to Lake Ann. The extra distance had proven to be exhausting for both of us. Best to keep this trip shorter.

The boys and I stopped at the White River ranger station for a permit. It was then that I discovered the popularity of Summerland. I had tried to avoid the weekend rush by heading in on a Sunday, when I thought most people would be leaving. We'd planned to stay two nights, but to my dismay, no empty campsites remained in the campground. Between Wonderland Trail hikers and people who hiked in to spend time enjoying the meadows at Summerland, the place was full.

Fortunately, the ranger offered us an alternative. "I could issue you a wilderness backcountry permit for the area just beyond Panhandle Gap."

"How much farther is that?" I asked.

"It's about another mile and a half from the campground to Pan Gap," the ranger replied. "You gain about 900 more feet in altitude. You can find a place to camp just on the other side. Just be sure you set up your tent far enough from the trail where no one can see it."

I asked the boys, "Do you think you can do that?"

"Sure," said Kris, always game for an adventure.

"I don't know," Tim said. "I guess so." He really didn't have a concept of what the suggestion meant, but he went along with his brother's enthusiasm.

I thought it over, and decided it was worth the effort. This was no time to turn around and go home. Great weather beckoned. Besides, our full backpacks waited for us in the car. I said to the ranger, "Sure. We'll take the permit."

As he filled out the paperwork, the ranger warned, "Be careful up there. A big cliff drops off that ridge. People have died up there."

Two pairs of eyes widened with astonishment. "Really?" Kris asked.

"Yes, there was this woman. She was some kind of botanist, or something. She was collecting plants and got too close to the edge."

"We'll be careful," I assured him as he handed me the permit. We headed out the door and drove up to the trailhead to start our hike.

At first the wide, well-used trail wandered through tall old-growth trees along Fryingpan Creek. Kris forged ahead like an old pro. Tim had trouble settling in to the hike. He wore a red kid-sized external frame backpack, but he couldn't get comfortable with the way it fit on his back.

"Mom, my hip belt hurts," he whined. I looked at his slender little body. He didn't have any fat to pad his hips.

"Here." I stopped. "Let me take your sleeping bag. I'll carry it."

Not much farther up the trail, I heard, "Mom, my shoulder straps are bugging me."

Tim felt every strap and belt and every ounce of weight in the pack, which held a couple of items of clothing, his sleeping pad, and his lunch.

I often told them stories as we hiked to distract them, but inspiration deserted me now. Then an idea struck. In my pack, I carried one of my favorite outdoor books, *Pecked to Death by Ducks* by Tim Cahill, a collection of outdoor essays. I'd brought it along thinking it would be fun to read one or two of the stories in the evening before bedtime. I hoped the boys would enjoy his humor and style of writing as much as I did.

We took another break and I dug out the book. "How would you like me to read to you while we hike?" I offered.

"Sure!" Kris said.

"I guess," Tim responded.

As we started up again, I picked out an essay to read to them as we plodded toward our destination. The story was about a man who stayed awake for twenty hours because the sound of a nearby grizzly frightened him. Then, when he finally saw the bear, he fell asleep lying under a nearby bush. Tim quit complaining and both boys enjoyed the story.

The trail was wide and relatively rock free for the first three miles or so. This made reading easy. I watched my footing with my peripheral vision and did a good job of staying upright. We were the target of many amused looks by Sunday hikers making their way back down the trail. I didn't care. It worked.

Once we reached the crossing of Fryingpan Creek, the trail grew narrower and rockier. I had to put the book away so I could watch for obstacles. By then both boys were engaged in the journey.

Soon we reached the last half mile of the trail—switchbacks that led up a steep hill to the campground. "When we get to the top of these, we'll be in Summerland," I encouraged them. Every time Tim asked how much farther, I'd respond, "Just a couple more switchbacks. We're almost there."

Finally, we reached the meadows of Summerland. From there we could see Mount Rainier rising into the deep-blue sky to the west, in all her spectacular glory. We could even pick out the climbing route on the Emmons Glacier above Camp Schurman.

A high-pressure weather system had recently parked over the region, bringing high temperatures with it. But in the mountains, we were able to escape the heat. We enjoyed temperatures that were ten to fifteen degrees cooler than the eighties and low nineties that people were experiencing in the lowlands.

Lupine, bistort, paintbrush, and heather covered in bright-pink blossoms decorated the hillsides. These, along with other bright flowers scattered across the green slopes of the meadows, always made Summerland resplendent in mid to late July. This day held true to form.

"Look, guys." I paused to point out a bright, rosy flower. "A magenta paintbrush!"

"Yeah, Mom," Kris humored me.

Tim just looked over and kept walking.

"And look, Tim. There's your flower—the mouse on a stick."

He perked up at that. "There's more over there." He pointed at a group of fuzzy-topped stems ahead of us.

After I'd pointed out a couple more types of flowers and still received little reaction, I got the message. They really didn't care.

We took a lunch break on a rock near a creek just beyond the camp, where we enjoyed the view. Then we picked up our packs and headed up the trail toward Panhandle Gap.

The landscape we walked through soon turned stark and barren. Where the trail works its way above the meadows near the Summerland campground, it crosses a field of boulders, and the slope rises up to a vertical cliff on the right. Mountain goats wander through various parts of the area, including the base of the cliff. As we toiled upward, we scoured the rocks and green patches above but didn't spot any.

A large log, flattened on top, formed a bridge where we crossed a stream of tumbling white water. Then the trail steepened again, winding through rocks and over pumice and sand. A few hardy plants sprinkled the arid ground, including partridge foot with its tiny white flowers and Davis's knotweed, a *Polygonum* whose leaves turn a vibrant red in late summer. The green meadows seemed far behind us. Then the incline eased as the trail meandered past a cold turquoise lake nestled against white snowfields at the base of the ridge rising above us. We took advantage of another great place to take a break.

Our last big challenge lay ahead. The trail grew steeper and eventually traversed one final snowy slope. We picked our way through an icy patch that rarely melted. Then we arrived at the saddle on the ridge—Panhandle Gap.

We had reached the highest point on the Wonderland Trail, where we took in the view of a broad green basin. Beyond a divide, in the next drainage over, Ohanapecosh Park formed a green oasis below the rugged ridges and glaciers of Mount Rainier. This distant valley was where the Indian Bar shelter and campground were nestled beside the Ohanapecosh River. Farther south, we spotted the jagged peaks of the Goat Rocks.

Looking back the way we came, we could still see Mount Rainier peeking out from behind the ridge we stood on. At the foot of Little Tahoma, the Fryingpan Creek basin extended to Goat Island Mountain.

Our backcountry permit allowed us to choose a campsite in the upper part of the basin beyond the pass. The ranger told us to find a spot below the saddle, somewhere that couldn't be seen from the trail. This would preserve the wilderness experience for hikers on the Wonderland Trail.

The boys rested and enjoyed the view, even finding Mount Adams on the horizon beyond the Goat Rocks. To our right, the rugged, snow-spotted ridge rose in a series of small summits, becoming part of the land of snow and ice. But we would be camping down below in a more hospitable landscape decorated with meadows. The snow patches had melted from the green ridge already, so no rushing streams tumbled through the sparse meadows.

I surveyed the terrain, looking for a place flat enough to pitch a tent with water available nearby. The sun continued to move steadily lower. We needed to pitch our tent and rest, then make dinner. Scrubby trees marched down steep slopes in long stringers, offering no protection or places to hide our tent. I searched until I spotted a flat area a couple hundred yards away with a promising depression nearby.

"I think I've found a spot," I told the boys, pointing. "See that grassy place? Get your packs on. We just have to go a little farther."

Tim picked up his pack with a groan, while Kris shrugged into his with no hesitation. We made our way down through rocky slopes and sparse patches of grass.

The first place we checked out seemed a little too visible from the trail. A nearby flat spot, partially hidden behind a rise in the terrain, looked more promising. Small pieces of pumice and sprinkles of grass covered the site. A scattering of rocks and grassy hummocks surrounded it. Above us, a slope rose to the trail. The nearby depression proved to be a tiny pool, the beginnings of a small stream. It was just big enough to provide our needed water.

"I think this will work," I told the boys.

"Good." Tim set his pack down and took off toward the little creek. "Maybe there are frogs in the water."

That evening, we made freeze-dried beef stroganoff for dinner. "What do you think?" I asked, as we ate out of the food preparation bags.

"It's good." Kris dipped his spoon in the bag again.

I turned to his brother. "What about you, Tim?"

"I like it," he admitted.

This dinner would become one of our backcountry favorites for several years.

At dusk, we nestled into our sleeping bags and I brought out my Tim Cahill book for another story. Afterward, I turned off my headlamp and the boys doused their flashlights. Despite the unfamiliar surroundings, we slept soundly in our little tent that night.

The second day greeted us with clear azure skies once again. After breakfast, I suggested we look for a different campsite farther from the trail. We explored along the ridge and found another saddle, this one covered with small pieces of pumice. Alpine plants and tough high-altitude grass grew in sparse patches. We approached the edge of the saddle with caution. On the Fryingpan Creek side, the ridge plunged down toward the creek below in a series of steep cliffs.

"Look down there." I pointed toward the valley bottom far below. "The trail we hiked on is right there on the other side of the creek."

"Really?" Kris said.

"Yeah, remember those cliffs we saw when we came up? This was one of them."

"That's a long way down," Tim said.

"It sure is," I agreed.

From this saddle, the ridge rose up again to the east, all cliffs on the Fryingpan side, with a grassy slope on our side. "These must be the cliffs the ranger warned us about." I gestured toward the steep escarpments.

"Why would anyone want to collect plants up here?" Kris asked.

"Lots of reasons." I pictured myself wandering around the meadows, looking at flowers and sticking samples between pieces of cardboard. It sounded idyllic.

We moved back from the cliff. Below the saddle we found a tiny stream flowing from a small spring adjacent to a flat grassy area. Magenta paintbrush and a sprinkling of lupines decorated the small meadow.

"How's this look, guys?" I asked. "It's farther from the trail, and it's a nice grassy spot."

They agreed it looked fine. We hiked back to the tent, gathered our belongings, and moved everything to our new site.

Before reestablishing camp, we took a lunch break. Our eyes again turned to the landscape that stretched to the horizon. Blue ridges faded into the distance. Kris said, "I don't see Mount Adams. Where'd it go?"

"I guess it disappeared into the smog," I answered. "This high-pressure system doesn't provide any wind to blow away the dirty air." This was one of their early meteorology lessons.

Tim gazed at the green slope above us. "What are those white things up there?" he asked. "I think they're moving!"

I looked where he pointed and saw small white figures in the meadow. "Those are mountain goats," I said. "There sure are a lot of them." We counted twelve to fifteen bucks and does, and even two or three kids. It was the largest herd I had ever seen.

"Can we go up there?" Kris asked with excitement. "I want to get closer."

"Yeah, Mom, can we?" Tim asked.

"I'd really like to get this tent set up," I said.

"We could go by ourselves," Kris pleaded.

"You'd have to be careful," I said. "You can't go anywhere near those cliffs."

"Yeah, Mom, we know," Kris assured me.

"And you shouldn't chase the goats. You can try to get closer, but don't make them run away. This is their home, and we shouldn't bother them."

After more promises to be careful, the boys set off through the grassy meadow and up the hillside toward the goats.

"Stay away from those cliffs!" I watched them take off on their expedition.

I scanned the hillside every so often, keeping an eye on their tiny figures, while I finished with the tent and wandered the meadow taking pictures of wildflowers. They returned a couple of hours later, ready to give me a report of their explorations.

"We decided to see how close we could get," Tim said, his eyes shining with excitement.

"Yeah," Kris said. "We moved slow and tried to be real sneaky, but when we got close, they started looking our way and moved off a little ways."

"So, then we tried it again. We really thought we were being careful," Tim added.

"But they still moved away before we got really close," Kris said.

"How many times did you do that?" I asked.

"Oh, three or four times," Kris said. "Then they just moved off a little faster and went too far away."

"But I found some goat hair!" Tim grinned and pulled a wad of white fuzz out of his pocket.

"That's cool," I said. "Just like in Glacier Basin."

"Then we decided to go up toward the top of the ridge," Tim said. "But we were careful and didn't get close to the cliff, like you said."

"Sounds like you had a good time." I was pleased they had been able to enjoy their time in this beautiful environment.

We crawled into our sleeping bags that night thinking about gleaming snow-covered mountains, green grass-covered slopes, mountain goats, and alpine flowers.

During the night, the weather in the region finally caught up with us. It was cool enough that we still used our sleeping bags to ward off the chill, but the heat of the lowlands brought us thunderstorms. Somewhere around midnight, I woke to the sound of a low growl in the distance. I lay listening as the sounds slowly grew louder. Soon the walls of the tent lit up dimly with the flicker of faraway lightning.

I counted the seconds between flashes and rumbles, reassured by how slowly the storm seemed to move toward our exposed campsite. I considered our location, which was fairly close to the depression where the tiny stream headed downhill, and wondered how much rain it would take to cause water to run through our tent. Still, I didn't feel any urgency to move our camp.

Soon, I sensed stirring beside me. Kris could sleep through a hurricane, but Tim woke to the clamor. "I hear thunder," he said. "Is it going to rain?"

"It might," I told him, "but it will probably pass over us quickly." Another meteorology lesson. "We're safe in the tent," I reassured him.

Another flash lit up the tent, followed soon by a deep rumble.

"Do you want to know how to tell how far away the lightning is?" I asked.

"Okay."

"When you see the light from the flash, start counting seconds—one-chimpanzee, two-chimpanzee, and so on. If you get to five chimpanzees, it's a mile away."

I showed him how it worked. Another flash, and I started counting. Finally, low grumbling reached us. "See, that was thirty chimpanzees. So, it was about six miles away. Not too close." We continued to count, but the lightning never came closer than five miles—twenty-five chimpanzees.

As rain started to spatter the walls of the tent, Tim's next concern became the hike out the next day. "What if it's raining tomorrow when we hike to the car?"

"We'll just hike through it," I told him. "Nothing to worry about. Even if we get wet, we have a warm car waiting for us, and dry clothes in our packs to change into. We'll be fine."

Before long, the rain ceased and the thunder faded into the distance. Feeling reassured, Tim's anxiety ebbed and he fell back to sleep.

When we opened our tent door the next morning on the slope below Panhandle Gap, a cloudless blue expanse greeted us. Tim's fears evaporated. We spread the tent out to dry, in no hurry to pack up our gear and start down the trail.

When we finally did head out, we stopped at the ranger station and told the ranger about the goat herd that wandered on the hillside. He smiled and thanked us for the report. Then he told us that people often saw goats on the ridges and in the meadows near Panhandle Gap.

Since our trip, I've looked for goats every time I return to that trail. I have often spotted them high on the skyline above the upper part of the trail, or somewhere beyond Panhandle Gap. Once, when I couldn't find the trail under the snow, I even followed goat tracks to guide me from the creek crossing above Summerland to Pan Gap.

Goats and meadows, explorations and stories. More threads woven into the tapestry of our family's outdoor adventures.

Our camping trip to Panhandle Gap wasn't the only time I found myself in a tent with Tim during a thunderstorm. Twenty-nine years later we would share a remarkable experience while taking a trip together to Southern Utah. We had planned to hike in the Grand Gulch area. But our plans changed when a series of rainstorms marched through the region, making the canyons dangerous and impassable. We still found places to explore, though, and on one of our last days in the area, we saw a sign pointing off to the east, directing us toward Bears Ears. We were curious since neither of us had ever seen the formation before.

We followed a sign up a dirt road that wound across a flat area dotted with piñons and junipers. Then it headed up the side of a mesa toward another higher bench. As I drove, I watched the road with caution, knowing that rain could cause many of these roads to become impassable. When we reached the top, we saw that the surrounding juniper and piñon pine forest would prevent any views of Bears Ears for several miles. We turned around and drove down a couple hundred feet to a well-used campsite perched high above the flat land below, in a corner of the road.

As we settled back with our dinners and hot drinks, we enjoyed a view whose panorama stretched from the southern to the western horizons. Above those far-off mountains, distant thunderclouds marched across the sky, lighting up with internal explosions.

I slept soundly that night until about six in the morning, when I woke to the sound of thunder. I snuggled in my sleeping bag and counted the seconds between flashes that lit up the tent and the subsequent grumbling thunder. Soon a patter of raindrops hit the tent, adding a staccato melody to the bass drum background. The time between flash and sound grew shorter and shorter until flashes and thunder were mixed together, coming from different directions in a confusing cacophony.

Tim woke as the din grew louder. He marveled with me as the raindrops turned into a downpour, adding a roar to the drumbeat of the thunder. I longed to stick my head out the door of the rainfly to watch the light show, but I knew I would get drenched in seconds, along with some of the gear in the tent. I continued to time the lightning and thunder, thinking about our exposed position on the hillside, but the interval never grew shorter than five chimpanzees—one mile away.

We knew the storm would pass, so we just stayed nestled in our sleeping bags, listening to the concert. After an hour or so, the sound of the rain slowly abated until it became a light patter again, and then only a drop here and there. When I sat up to make my way outside, I noticed a wet tent floor under my sleeping pad. Later, as we folded up the tent, we found trails made by water flowing under our tent floor—small streams that had followed the paths of least resistance.

I had experienced thunderstorms in a tent a few times before, but this was definitely the most violent. The sky had thrown everything it had at us. But unlike our trip to Summerland, this time Tim didn't need my reassurances that the storm would pass. Both with and without me, he had gathered enough experience over the years to build his confidence and weather the storm.

STEPPING STONES

I will prepare and some day
my chance will come.

—Abraham Lincoln

Kris had eyed the summit of Mount Rainier for a long time. The climbing bug had initially bit him during his first back- packing trip in 1986. He'd stood on the shores of Lake Ann looking at Mount Shuksan and told me he was going to climb that mountain someday. But over the next few years, his goal had shifted.

As he observed my first attempts to reach the top of Mount Rainier, his determination had really taken hold. He decided he would conquer Mount Rainier by the time he turned sixteen. Over the years, he'd watched me take climbing trips in the Cascades every summer, adding summits of Mount Rainier, Mount Baker, Mount Adams, and other Cascade peaks to my list of accomplishments. His envy and resolve had grown with each of my expeditions.

As the summer of 1994 approached, Kris spent considerable time trying to convince me he was capable of attempting his first summit climb of Mount Rainier. He would turn fifteen in August and he felt his self-imposed deadline creeping up on him.

I was now five feet, four inches tall. Who knew you could grow as an adult? For some reason, maybe because of all the stretching I'd done during my rock climbing escapades, I'd gained an inch in the last couple of years. Still, Kris had overtaken me in height and added a few more inches on top of that. The blond hair of his toddler years had long since darkened to a medium brown.

Whenever the opportunity came up for him to tag along on the self-arrest training sessions I taught or participated in, he jumped at the chance. But his body had yet to fill out into a sturdy adult shape, and maternal caution caused me to hesitate. I wasn't ready to concede that he was prepared to tackle the upper mountain.

As a compromise, I finally said, "How about I take you to Camp Schurman in late July? You can find out what it's like on a glacier."

"I guess," he said with subdued excitement. "But I really want to try to get to the top."

"I know. Let's see how you do on this trip."

Camp Schurman on the northeast flank of Mount Rainier, and Camp Muir on the south side, are stepping stones along the two most popular routes to climb Mount Rainier. Clark Schurman had been the chief climbing guide in the Park from 1939 to 1942. He'd long dreamed of a shelter cabin at Steamboat Prow, but he had already passed away by the time his dream came to fruition in 1955.

To reach Camp Schurman, which sits at 9,460 feet, Kris and I planned to hike through Glacier Basin, then navigate Inter Glacier and cross a small portion of the Emmons Glacier.

"Not only will you get to see real crevasses," I told him, "but you'll find out how tough it is to climb to high altitudes with a heavy pack full of gear."

"How long are we going to stay at Camp Schurman?" he asked.

"You know how I usually spend my first night at Glacier Basin and then head up to Camp Schurman on the second day when I climb? Let's do that," I suggested. "We'll just stay up high for one night."

"We'll hike out in one day?" he asked.

"Yes, it'll be a lot easier going downhill."

The weather blessed us with cloudless skies as we hefted our packs and started up the trail. Kris enthusiastically led the way through trees and flower-strewn meadows. After three and a half miles, we arrived at the Glacier Basin campground. We pitched our tent in a designated site and then followed the path to the meadow to watch climbers come down the trail from higher ground.

After a bit, I pointed up to the hill on the right. "Look up there. See if you can spot any mountain goats."

We scoured the hillside and cliffs to our right, below the massive basalt buttress where the goats often hung out.

"I don't see any," Kris said, after a thorough search.

"They must be hiding," I said. "Let's go organize our camp. Then we can eat dinner."

Later, we poured boiling water into our bag of freeze-dried spaghetti. "This is really good." Kris had a hard time waiting while I took my turn digging a spoonful out of the foil bag. Over the years, as the boys and I had shared dinners, we learned to avoid dirty dishes by eating straight out of the package.

Light faded into darkness and we settled into our tents to grab a few hours of sleep. Thoughts of the next day's challenge crowded our minds but didn't keep us awake long.

The next morning, we rose early and heated water for oatmeal and hot cocoa.

"Are you ready for this, Kris?"

"Sure. Let's go."

Gear already stashed, we hefted the packs onto our backs and started the next leg of our adventure.

The trail headed straight across the nearby meadow and then worked its way up a ridge—a lateral moraine made of hard yellow clay covered with loose dirt and small volcanic rocks. This steep section that hikers called the yellow hill puts many a climber on their butt when they descend.

Where the steepest part begins, the left side of the ridge drops off precipitously toward a raging creek eighty feet below, fed by meltwater from snow patches and glacier ice. Cold blue water foams and swirls between the rocks and boulders that blanket the valley floor. For several steps along the ridge, whiffs of sulfur serve as a reminder that this mountain is indeed volcanic.

Once we'd conquered the yellow hill, we followed the wandering trail through the rocky upper reaches of Glacier Basin. Then we arrived at the bottom of Inter Glacier, which rose steeply toward the sky.

"Let's stop for a break," I suggested.

"Sounds good." Kris set down his pack on a nearby rock and rummaged for his snack bag.

"Grab your sunscreen while you're at it," I advised. "We'll want to put more on before we get on the snow."

We needed the extra protection since we were climbing under a clear azure sky, the sunlight intense as it reflected off the bright snow surface. Kris wore a white climber's hat with long sides and a back flap that draped down to protect his neck. With his hat and dark glacier glasses, he looked the part of a real climber.

Because our route crossed glaciers, I carried a token short length of rope so Kris and I could tie together. Shorter and lighter than a standard climbing rope, it would still allow us to say we were roped up. Many parties rope up for Inter Glacier, but my experience on the route included several occasions when those in my party hadn't bothered. The previous winter, a heavy accumulation of snow had built up and much of it still remained, so I didn't worry about big crevasses now. Nevertheless, Kris and I tied together to give him the experience of traveling on rope, matching his pace to a partner's, and moving with an ice axe.

The route started up the right side of the glacier. This first slope was the steepest of the whole climb to Camp Schurman. I knew it could be treacherous, especially later in the season when the surface snow melted off and the slope turned icy. I'd been camping in Glacier Basin one August when rescuers had rushed to the bottom of the glacier. They'd had to camp overnight before they could evacuate a descending climber who'd slipped and crashed into the rocks along the edge of the icy slope and broke his femur.

The trail soon cut over to the center of the glacier. About halfway up the glacier, shortly before the top of the steepest section eased off, Kris slipped and put his self-arrest skills to use. If he had gone zipping down the hill, I would have been hard pressed to stop him with the short length of rope that tied us together. But thanks to his previous practice and a snowy surface that had softened in the sun, he quickly stopped himself.

"Good job!" I called. "You did great."

I looked down the steep grade. *It really isn't that dangerous here*, I thought. *Even if we'd gone sliding down the steep snow, we would have been able to stop ourselves down there near the bottom where it eases off.*

As we ascended, Kris enjoyed new experiences. He encountered crevasses for the first time and easily stepped across them. These unimposing cracks were only four to six inches wide. Though narrow, they appeared to be bottomless and stretched for many yards in length across the snowy slope.

About two-thirds of the way up the glacier, we crossed to the left side. Suddenly, we heard shouting off to our right. Muffled sounds of "Stop!" and loud whistles caught our attention. We saw several climbers below us frantically waving. Shouts of warning echoed as a lone figure glissaded down the upper part of the wedge-shaped glacier, immediately below Steamboat Prow.

This direct route went straight up and down and could sometimes be safely navigated early in the season. But as summer progressed, and the sun melted the snow cover, crevasses tended to open up early in that part of Inter Glacier.

The climbers below on the glacier could see what the glissader, sliding on his butt down the slope, couldn't. Not far below him, the slope curved down into a steeper section and dropped directly into a yawning crevasse that bisected the icy glacier.

Whether the sliding man heard the warnings or realized himself that danger lay ahead, he managed to arrest his slide shortly before the drop that would have sent him plunging into the crevasse. Kris and I couldn't hear the sighs of relief coming from the people scattered across the glacier under the intense blue sky that day, but we knew we all felt the same.

We continued up the left side of the glacier to 8,700 feet, where we reached the ridge leading up to Steamboat Prow. This was just below Camp Curtis, a rarely used site that looked like a small group of rock rings. Instead of following the ridge up, however, we crossed it and dropped down to the Emmons Glacier. It was during the descent to the glacier that Kris experienced his tensest moments of the whole day.

As I led Kris down a steep slope of soft dirt and pebbles, each step made us feel like we were in jeopardy. Along the trail, short sections of unstable mud created by meltwater interrupted the path. No longer firm, the muck gave way as it sucked at our boots. We had to work hard to stay on the trail. Below us, big holes gaped between the edge of the glacier and the sun-warmed dirt and rocks of the ridge. They threatened to swallow us if we made a misstep.

At the bottom of the slope, one of these chasms greeted us. We needed to get to the dirty surface of the glacier on the other side. "You're going to have to take an extra big step to get across this," I warned Kris. "It's not too wide. You shouldn't have any trouble." I sounded more confident than I felt about crossing with my short legs.

Kris's trusting reply came quickly. "I can do it."

We tied the safety rope between us. I went first. Once across, I planted an ice axe to serve as an anchor on the other side, to guard against a fall. I wrapped the rope around it and asked, "Are you ready?"

"Yeah." Kris hesitated, then took a giant step. I kept the rope taut as he moved, helping with his momentum.

"That was pretty scary," he admitted once he stood on my side of the crevasse.

"You did a great job. Hopefully, that will be the only one we have to cross that way."

We then made our way up the Emmons to Camp Schurman. Along the way, we skirted a couple of large yawning crevasses that descended into turquoise-blue depths. Crossing a few smaller openings in the snow seemed like a cakewalk in comparison. We took turns placing standing anchors with our ice axes as one person yelled, "Crossing!" and then jumped across while the other person watched alertly. The hut the rangers used was visible above us, a solid stone edifice etched against the sky.

After about a half hour on the glacier, we reached the flat rocky spit of black volcanic sand and gravel near the hut. This saddle, which sits below Steamboat Prow, marks the beginning of the separation between the Emmons and the Winthrop Glaciers.

In 1994, midweek traffic to the camp was still light enough for us to easily find a site on the flat sandy area and not have to sleep on snow. Knowing this, I planned accordingly. It helped that we'd arrived at a time between the departure of many parties who'd already climbed and the arrival of others who planned to ascend that night.

In the early afternoon sunlight, we found several available sites, each big enough for a tent and cook area.

"Which one looks the best to you?" I asked Kris.

"That one looks great." He pointed to a sandy area sprinkled with small pieces of pumice. Black rocks piled two to three feet high surrounded the site. The wall they formed served as a rudimentary windbreak.

We set about erecting our tent.

"Pull out those guylines attached to the rainfly and tie each of them to a rock," I directed. I set to work tying out the corners of the tent.

"Do I have to do them all?" Kris eyed the eight cords tied to tabs on the rainfly.

"You sure do. It can get windy up here, even when the weather is good." Having been at Camp Schurman with winds howling at over a hundred miles per hour, I knew that unanticipated strong winds frequently streamed across the pass. I didn't want to take any chances.

Once I finished securing the tent corners, I helped Kris with the guylines. We piled several rocks on top of the anchors for added security. When we finished, the tent looked like a fat yellow bug caught in a crazy spider web.

By the time evening arrived, other climbing parties filled the adjacent sites. Tents sprouted up on the nearby Winthrop Glacier like multicolored mushrooms.

Camping on the Winthrop at Camp Schurman doesn't present much danger. The slope of the glacier moderates, so falling isn't a factor. Most people who make it to the camp have plenty of experience sleeping on snow. With time and effort, a person can shovel out a flat platform for their tent, creating a good place to set up a temporary home. But conditions change from year to year, so a climber has to be careful and observant. It is, after all, a glacier.

A few years after this trip with Kris, I camped on the Winthrop at a time when the snow on the upper mountain wasn't as deep as usual. During the day, our group noticed several small crevasses that extended across the snow slope and down toward the camp area. Every so often during those three days, one of us would go out and use a shovel to knock down the sides of the larger nearby cracks. A few of them widened to as much as twelve inches, or even bigger. We wanted to make them obvious so they didn't take anyone by surprise.

On the second day, a member of our party noticed a crevasse aimed straight for the tent of two other camp residents. The occupants of the tent noticed it, too, when they came back from a scouting trip. A few hours later, after seeing that the crack had thrust all the way under their tent to the other side, they quickly moved to a different site.

I always found it easier to camp on dry land if an open space remained available.

Once our tent was in place, Kris and I threw our sleeping bags and pads inside. "It's a good thing you don't sleepwalk," I told him. "If you took off in that direction, look where you'd go." I pointed toward the Emmons. From the camp area, the rocky saddle dropped off abruptly. A hapless wanderer would plunge into a huge gap where the rock wall met the glacier below. "You wouldn't survive that."

Kris walked over to the edge, about fifteen feet away. "Wow," he said. "That would be horrible."

"And if you wandered that way"—I pointed to the slope heading away from camp toward the mountain's summit—"you'd reach crevasses that crisscross the whole route. If you weren't tied to a partner, you'd probably just disappear."

"What if I headed over there?" Kris pointed toward the tents on the Winthrop. "Those people set up their tents on the glacier."

"Yeah, it's safe close to the dirt here, but if you made it beyond the camping area, you'd start running into more crevasses pretty soon.

"Face it," I added. "At Camp Schurman, sleepwalking would probably be deadly."

After we finished setting up camp, I suggested, "Let's go over and see Gator."

We made our way to the stone hut where the twenty-four-year-old climbing ranger, Mike Gauthier, made his home. Called "Gator" by his friends, the square-jawed, dark-haired man with blue eyes already had four years of experience as a climbing ranger under his belt.

I had met him the year before, and we'd instantly formed a friendship based on our shared love of the mountains. We easily fell into friendly banter as we shared our experiences in the outdoors.

Mike later went on to become the head climbing ranger in Mount Rainier National Park and continued to advance in the Park Service beyond that. In 2004, *Men's Journal* would name him one of the 25 Toughest Men in America, thanks in part to his climbing and rescue exploits. He's also written a climbing guide for Mount Rainier. In the years I've known him, though, fame never changed him. He has always possessed a thoughtful, generous personality and a wonderful sense of humor.

It was great to see him. Never stingy with his smile, Gator greeted us with a grin that reached every part of his face. Tall and slim, he wore a short-sleeved gray park uniform shirt and dark-green shorts that showed off his fitness. "You should have told me you were coming. You could have stayed in the hut with me."

"That's okay," I responded. "This way Kris gets to experience what climbing up here is really like."

Gator invited us into the hut and gave us a tour. Of course, I'd been there before, during my experience when we encountered the wind storm, but this was Kris's first visit. Also, I was interested in the details a ranger could offer. Gator explained to Kris that a group of local climbers had completed the hut at Camp Schurman in 1961 as a shelter to be used in bad weather. Climbing rangers used it now as a base of operations on the east side of Mount Rainier. It looked just as I remembered it—a very large corrugated culvert with about a third of it cut off so it could be set on its side. Rocks had been cemented all over the surface, and wooden walls built on each end. One window was built into the end facing the sheer cliff of the Prow. The wall with the door and another window faced the Emmons and Winthrop Glaciers flowing down Mount Rainier.

I noticed more details this time as Gator pointed out the short ladder beyond the bunks on the left that led up to a trapdoor and the attic. He explained that rangers stored rescue equipment there. "When we have a full house," he said, "there's even room to squeeze in a couple more sleeping spots up there." It had been locked when we took shelter in the hut in 1988.

The bunk I had stayed in had been replaced by cupboards. The gas stove still stood in its place on the counter at the far end.

"Have a seat." He motioned to a bunk near the door.

Kris and I plopped onto the sagging canvas and leaned back against the wall.

"How was your hike up?"

We filled him in, enjoying this encounter with civilization.

"There was this guy who almost slid into a crevasse!" Kris said with excitement.

"Yeah," I added, "he was glissading down from the Prow and almost didn't stop before that big crevasse that crosses the glacier."

We told him about the people yelling and waving, and how that seemed to catch the guy's attention.

"I can't believe some of the things people do up here." Gator shook his head. "And the crazy thing is, they usually get away with it."

After catching up with the ranger, Kris and I headed back to our site to melt water and fix our freeze-dried dinner packet.

As we approached our tent, we noticed a couple of strong young men setting up a yellow, dome-shaped North Face mountaineering tent between our site and the Emmons drop-off. They wore the usual climbing attire, including dark long-sleeved polypro shirts, pants with generous pockets, and well-worn, clunky climbing boots.

A short, sandy-haired man with a wiry build worked beside his tall, stocky companion. Their ruddy faces showed evidence of days spent in the sun. We noticed the characteristic "rac-coon eyes" of climbers—pale skin around the eyes—when the shorter man briefly took off his sunglasses. I soon realized they were talking in German.

I took a couple of steps toward their site. "Hi, how are you guys doing?"

The shorter guy said, "Hi," with a smile and a nod. That seemed to exhaust his English vocabulary.

"Do you happen to be from Germany? I have a friend who lives in Freiburg."

The taller man answered in thickly accented English and confirmed they were indeed German.

"Are you planning to go to the top?" I asked.

"Yes, tonight."

"I didn't see you come up the Emmons. Did you come over the Prow?"

"No, we came over the Winthrop Glacier." He gestured to the west, then explained in his thick accent, "We left our car at Sunrise and hiked over to Curtis Ridge because we planned to climb Liberty Ridge." Sunrise was a tourist destination where a visitor center provided people with information, souvenirs, and lunch options. The lodge and parking lot were perched high on a ridge and served as a hub for several trails. "But when we got over to the Carbon Glacier," he said, "we saw there was too much falling rock and ice. It was too dangerous, so we hiked back and came up the Winthrop Glacier to here."

All in one day. Kris and I exchanged glances, impressed. We realized these guys had to be pretty strong, and obviously they knew something about climbing.

"You made a good decision," I said. "This late in the summer, it gets pretty bad over there. People usually attempt that route in May or early June."

The Liberty Ridge route had become a well-known climber's destination after it was described in a book, *Fifty Classic Climbs of North America*. Along with the increase in attempts on this route came a rise in deaths. The route is best attempted in late spring, before the summer weather melts the ice holding loose rocks in place. But even then, other hazards can make the route treacherous. Storms can bring heavy snow to the mountain, increasing the avalanche danger. Climbers have been buried in their tents, dying of suffocation when their efforts to keep their tents clear couldn't keep up with the deepening blanket.

The Germans seemed anxious to get back to their camp duties, so I said, "Well, good luck." Kris and I headed back to our camp to start preparing our supper.

By six o'clock, many of the inhabitants of the camp had already crawled into their sleeping bags, wanting to rest up before starting their climbs in the middle of the night. Others weren't far behind and by eight, few voices could be heard besides Kris's and mine.

Still on a normal sleep schedule, Kris and I talked quietly. I searched my backpack until I found a deck of cards, and we settled in for a few games of cribbage. Unfortunately, tent walls don't stop sound. At least one person nearby found our whispers and quiet chuckles too loud. We heard a *"Shh!"* and a soft "Quiet down" through the thin walls of our tent. We grinned and shrugged and continued with a few more games, lowering our voices to soft whispers and making fewer comments as we played.

By ten o'clock, we too had curled up in our sleeping bags. Soon after that we heard the first sounds of people unzipping their tents so they could crawl out and get ready for their summit attempts. For the next three hours we intermittently dozed and listened to the sounds of murmuring voices and hissing stoves as different groups melted snow for water. These noises were punctuated by the jingle of climbing equipment being arranged.

As midnight grew close and darkness smothered the camp, we also had to put up with flashlights illuminating our tent every few minutes. Along with the annoying lights flashing across our tent walls, we heard murmuring.

One comment came through clearly. "You know, those guys at the site over there left early because of all the talking coming from that small tent."

Is that really true? I wondered with chagrin.

Finally, around one o'clock, the last party left for the summit and Kris and I fell into a sound sleep. We never heard the Germans leave.

Around six the next morning, I got up long enough to make a trip to the outhouse. Though the sun's rays hadn't reached our tent yet, the route up the mountain was clearly laid out above me. Strings of climbers dotted the route up the Corridor, a section of unbroken glacier with crevasse fields on both sides. This feature started above Emmons Flats and led straight up the mountain to about 11,000 feet. The route up the mountain changes from day to day, week to week, and year to year, as glaciers move and crevasses open up and are covered again with snow. Yet, whatever direction the route takes, the Corridor invariably forms part of it.

When the rope teams reached the top of the Corridor, they angled across a traverse. They worked their way around several crevasses and finally reached the bergschrund—a large crevasse at the top of a mountain where the glacier ice separates from the stable snow above and starts flowing downslope. Once they crossed it, they disappeared over the last rise before the summit.

One particular party of two ascending the top of the Corridor, about halfway up the mountain, caught my eye. Their swift pace marked them as exceptional. In the short time I spent watching them, they gained on another rope team and quickly passed them.

I wriggled back into my sleeping bag for a few more minutes of slumber. Kris and I woke around eight o'clock to more bright sun and a stiff breeze. We crawled out of our tent and I checked all of our tent anchors. Everything looked secure, just as we'd left it.

Just then, a commotion about fifty yards or so out on the Winthrop Glacier caught our attention. A bright-yellow tent, anchored to the snow at only one corner, was on its side, rocking in a stiff breeze that threatened to pull its tenuous tether loose and send it tumbling across the glacier.

Two people rushed toward it, grabbed it, and pulled it back in place so they could put in more secure anchors. As we glanced around at other tents, Kris and I noticed that most climbers hadn't taken the time to use the extra anchor attachments on their rainflies, leaving the tents vulnerable to the notorious Camp Schurman winds. Several people were working to put extra anchors into the snow or add rocks on top of their stakes.

We glanced at the German men's tent and realized it needed help, too—and soon. Despite being such competent climbers, they didn't seem to have had much experience with the volcanic rocks on the flanks of Mount Rainier. These rocks are much lighter, comparatively, than granite and other rocks typically found on a mountainside.

The thin cords attached to the tent's corners were tied around six- or eight-inch-diameter rocks, totally inadequate anchors for the winds that commonly blew over the pass between the Emmons and Winthrop Glaciers. Their tent had been pushed to the very edge of the site and leaned toward the Emmons, preparing itself for a plunge into oblivion.

We hurried over, recentered the tent, then gathered rocks from the surrounding protective wall and piled them onto their anchors.

About an hour later, we watched two men roped together descend the last slope down to the camp area. Kris and I recognized them as the German climbers, returning ahead of almost all the other descending groups. We greeted them as they approached their site.

"When did you guys head up?" I asked.

"We left camp at four," their spokesman replied. They set their packs down on the ground.

Kris looked at his watch. "That's just five hours!"

We looked at each other with wide eyes. This confirmed our assessment of their climbing skills.

"Wow! You guys are really fast!" Kris said.

They smiled diffidently, but before they could turn to start packing, we told them about the wind and what we had done with their tent. They expressed quiet appreciation.

Soon they had packed up their gear and headed to their car, parked at Sunrise. That's when we put it all together.

"Wow!" Kris exclaimed. "They hiked from Sunrise to the base of Liberty Ridge, back to the Winthrop, and up here. Then they made it to the summit and came back down in five hours."

"And now they're headed back to Sunrise," I added. "All in about thirty-six hours."

"Boy, those guys are animals!" Kris announced. From that moment on, we referred to them as the "German animals."

We spent the morning watching climbing groups return from the summit and pack up their camps to head to their cars. Others came up the Emmons, set up camp, and got ready for their ascent attempts.

Our closest neighbors returned from their successful summit attempt and started breaking down their tent. I heard one of them comment, "I'm really exhausted."

As soon as their tent was stowed away, his partner headed to the outhouse. I approached the tired climber.

"I'm sorry for keeping you up last night. We didn't mean to be noisy."

"Oh, no! You didn't keep me awake. It was the mice that got in the tent and kept running over my face that didn't let me sleep!"

We shared a laugh. I felt better now about my bedtime card games with Kris.

After lunch we packed our gear and took off, retracing our steps down the Emmons and toward the ridge where we crossed over to Inter Glacier. We looked forward to the sections of the glacier where we could slide on our butts and enjoy the speed of the steep descent.

Before long, we angled up the trail that took us off the Emmons and roped up to head down through the first section of snow. Climbers dotted the glacier below us. As we descended, we met many of them heading up to camp, while others were people who had headed down before us. Most had followed the general route that we were taking—starting high on the right side of the glacier, then crossing about a third of the way down to the left side and finally heading straight down. This route avoided most of the crevasse fields.

Kris and I continued our descent, at times plunge stepping—digging our heels into the soft snow. We stepped over small crevasses that appeared periodically. Sometimes we took advantage of a chance to use a sitting glissade, sliding our way quickly down the glacier on our butts.

Kris led the way and I followed, tethered to him with our short rope. Near the bottom of our last glissade, I was surprised to see Kris's slide path go directly across a small gap. When I followed, I looked down into the blue depths, the beginnings of a crevasse. The three-inch-wide bottomless crack in the snow didn't present any real danger.

At the bottom of the snowfield, we stopped to rest and pack away our climbing gear and rope. We sat for a short while, eating granola bars and drinking in the sun and scenery of Upper Glacier Basin. After committing the views to memory, we continued our descent.

Hiking the trail down from Glacier Basin always seemed to take forever. Our bodies ached with fatigue and we craved salt, liquids, and "real" food. But the slow pace gave us time to transition back to civilization. That day, Kris and I left the mountain with another adventure under our belts, more great memories of a shared experience, and dreams of future climbs taking shape in our minds.

Summer 1995 arrived and Kris had yet to step on the summit of Mount Rainier. He would turn sixteen in August, and his eyes were still set on the goal he had made for himself years before.

I hadn't yet organized a climb that Kris could join, but I decided to take Gator up on the offer he'd made the year before. We arranged a time in early July when Kris and I could head to Camp Schurman and stay in the ranger hut. At least that would feed his longing to reach higher elevations. Since we had no need to carry tents or any of the extra gear required for a summit attempt, we planned to hike to Schurman in one day.

Under deep-blue skies, Kris and I took a route to the climber's camp that I had never followed before. I had always hiked up to the head of Glacier Basin and then worked my way up Inter Glacier before dropping down on the Emmons Glacier or plodding straight up to Steamboat Prow. This time, we followed a different route that helped us avoid glaciers entirely. Gator had described it to me the year before, explaining that it was a route the rangers often took to avoid glacier travel when they hiked solo to the hut.

The first leg of the trip followed the established trail to the campground at Glacier Basin. After that, instead of heading up the yellow hill, we dropped over a bank on the left, down onto the rocky floor of the valley. We boulder-hopped across the rushing waters of Inter Fork Creek. The icy water had only minutes before escaped from the snow melting in the upper part of the basin. It formed a swirling torrent laced with white foam that curled back on itself. Then we crossed the broad valley to the base of the ridge on the other side of the creek. Traces of old abandoned roads, rusty sheet-metal boxes, and huge gears still remained to remind us of the copper miners who had abandoned their mining attempts many years ago.

We saw hints of a trail on the sloping side of the ridge ahead and aimed for a stringer of scrub junipers that ran up the steep hillside. When we reached the base of the slope, we found footprints and crushed vegetation, traces of a trail where rangers and other climbers had hiked. We followed the signs up faint switchbacks through the dwarf junipers and across the steep, rocky slope, and ascended steadily to the top of the ridge.

At first, the ridgetop seemed barren. Windblown and exposed, it was a place where no trees could take root. But small alpine plants grew close to the ground. Their tough, thick leaves were designed to soak up sunshine and conserve heat. Pussy-paws, Davis's knotweed, and fringe cup flourish in this type of environment.

Kris and I took a look over the other side of the ridge where the rocky tongue of the Emmons Glacier flowed far below us. A couple of turquoise lakes dotted the surface of the debris-covered glacier. Next, we turned uphill to follow the ridge toward Mount Ruth and, beyond it, Mount Rainier. Though its designation as a mountain makes it sound imposing, Mount Ruth is a just a little peak on the ridge that leads up to Steamboat Prow. Still, it's an obstacle that needed to be overcome.

At a spot before the path steepened, we skirted a rugged, hodgepodge group of rocks. Previous visitors had constructed a couple of crude tent shelters nearby in flat areas nestled against a yellow-brown rock wall. Climbers had stacked rocks on top of each other to form walls on the sides and front. These curved around in a semicircle meant to provide a tent with a measure of protection from the wind.

Beyond the tent sites, the route steepened. The traces of trail we followed directed us to the right and skirted the summit of Mount Ruth. In some places, we scrambled from rock to rock across loose talus slopes. We soon learned we had to test the stability of each rock before placing our weight on it.

Sometimes they rocked and knocked against each other with a hollow *clunk-clunk*. Sometimes they gave way beneath our feet and started sliding down the slope. We did our best to avoid those. Happy to finally see the end of that challenge, we rested before tackling the last obstacle between us and familiar ground.

Beyond Mount Ruth, the narrow trail skirted a rock wall high above the Emmons Glacier. As we worked our way along the route, Kris and I came to a place where the ledge we followed came to an abrupt halt. To proceed, we had to step across a large gap to a rock that jutted out from the wall ahead of us. It was perhaps less than eighteen inches across. But when we looked down to the glacier far below, it seemed like our stride would have to stretch across a yard or more. The fact that we carried full packs made the whole experience even more intimidating.

I watched with butterflies in my stomach as Kris found handholds on the rock beside him, and then stepped across to the other side. *Whew! I haven't killed my firstborn son.* Then I took my turn crossing the yawning chasm. *Big sigh of relief!*

After a few steps more around a corner, we came out on the saddle where the standard approach trails diverged. This was where we had dropped down onto the Emmons Glacier the year before, after reaching the top of Inter Glacier. Instead of heading down to the Emmons, we took an alternate trail that headed up the last part of the ridge to Steamboat Prow.

The trail was straightforward and followed a well-beaten track up the ridge through black volcanic rocks and sandy pumice. We passed Camp Curtis, an exposed area on the barren ridge where climbers occasionally set up their tents short of Camp Schurman.

Kris and I enjoyed the outstanding view as we gained altitude, one step at a time, toward the highest point of Steamboat Prow. Mount Rainier towered above the Emmons Glacier on our left. We could see the full length of the Emmons, from its source near the top of the mountain down to Camp Schurman. Blue crevasses crisscrossed its steep, snowy surface. Once below the camp, the slope of the glacier eased considerably. Pristine white turned to gray, and dark crevasses gaped below us along the cliff, occasionally reaching out across the surface of the ice. The steep slope on our left turned into a cliff, dropping off to the surface of the glacier below.

A couple hundred yards from the top of the Prow, we stopped and took our packs off, ready for another break.

I squinted up toward the mountain. "Look, Kris. See those groups of climbers?" I pointed to a string of little dots moving in sync as they descended the lower part of the mountain face.

Kris searched the slope. "Oh, I see them." He continued to scan the white glacier. "I see four rope teams scattered from there"—he pointed about halfway up the mountain—"all the way down to Camp Schurman."

"That's one more than I found," I admitted.

He pointed out the groups he'd spotted, and then I saw them, too.

"Let's see, there are three in that rope team, four in that one . . . ," he continued tallying up the climbers. "I came up with fourteen."

"That seems like a lot to be still coming down this time of day, but I trust you."

On our right, Inter Glacier descended toward Glacier Basin. Climbers below us worked their way slowly up the snowfield. Across the deep valley we had so recently escaped, a rocky ridge rose, sweeping down to a blue tree-covered area. We picked out the road to the visitor center and lodge at Sunrise, which was perched near the top of the tree line.

We got going again and I spotted a tiny little wildflower about three inches high, an alpine version of Cusick's speedwell blooming in this high, barren, rocky environment. "Look, Kris," I exclaimed. "Sky pilot!"

He murmured something unintelligible and kept plodding. He didn't feel the same thrill I did when I saw these special little blossoms. In my mind, the beauty of their small, dark-blue flowers with long, bright-yellow stamens was an act of defiance directed at the hostile terrain.

As we approached the high point of Steamboat Prow, my heart filled with emotion. The sounds of Aaron Copland's "Fanfare for the Common Man" filled the earphones I'd attached to a small cassette player I carried. The stirring music helped emphasize the grandeur around us and added to the sense of accomplishment I felt.

Finally, only one last test awaited us. At the top of the Prow, Kris and I found ourselves about two hundred feet above the Camp Schurman area. We needed to work our way down to the saddle between the Winthrop and Emmons Glaciers, where the ranger hut was solidly planted. This meant we had to drop down about fifty feet along a crude, narrow trail that was slippery with sand and loose pebbles, to the top of a steep, rocky slope.

Then we had to scramble down through rocks steep enough that the only way to safely descend was to face into the wall and use both hands and feet. I went first. "Don't follow too closely," I warned Kris. "If you knock a rock loose, I don't want it to hit me in the head."

With our packs threatening to throw us off balance, we took turns lowering ourselves from rock knob to crevice, from tiny ledge to sloping boulder slab. We placed each hand and foot carefully, testing the stability of the rocks as we went.

Once I worked my way down about ten feet and over to the right, I shouted, "Okay, you can follow now."

"Here I come."

As we continued to work our way down, I managed to stay far enough to one side or the other to avoid the sand and small rocks that Kris's boots dislodged.

I savored a feeling of relief when we both reached the bottom. Now we could relax and head to the ranger hut, a welcome shelter in a world of loose black rock and treacherous white ice.

When we got to the hut, we found an open door. I stuck my head in and spotted Gator in the dark interior, which seemed even darker after the white sunshine-blasted world we'd just left.

"Hi, Gator! We made it!"

Gator greeted us heartily and motioned us in. We eased off our packs and sat down gratefully on a bunk.

"How was your hike up?" Gator asked.

"It was great," Kris replied. "Though that step across the gap was pretty scary."

"That talus on Mount Ruth sure is loose," I said. "We thought we were going to start the whole hillside sliding a couple of times."

"You have to be careful on it, that's for sure," Gator agreed. "It can be pretty dangerous."

We shared more details about our hike up.

"I brought some things along that I think you'll like." From the top of my pack, I pulled out a cardboard cup wrapped in a sandwich bag. "Fresh blueberries. I'll make us some blueberry pancakes in the morning."

Gator's eyes opened wide in surprise, and his face lit up with amusement. The year before, he'd made an offhand comment about people who came up to stay in the hut and didn't contribute anything. I knew that nothing made it to the hut unless someone had carried it in, and I had been determined to bring him something he would truly enjoy.

"I also brought something else to share," I added with a grin. "You told me you had an oven in the hut, so I brought all the fixings to make a pizza."

Although I'd brought the ingredients, I really had no idea what kind of oven would work in the hut.

He laughed at my announcement and gave me a skeptical look.

"It's just a camp oven," he said. "It sits on top of the stove and it's not very big. I don't know how you could make pizza in it." He showed me a small metal box sitting on the back of the stove, only about a foot square and a little taller than it was wide.

Not ready to give up, I said, "We'll see. How about I make it tomorrow for dinner?"

"Sure, you can give it a try." The doubt in his voice was clear.

After we'd caught up on each other's lives, Gator said, "Would you like to see where you're going to sleep?"

"Sure," Kris said.

"If you go up the ladder"—Gator gestured toward the trap-door next to the wall—"there's room on the floor of the attic where you can spread out your sleeping bags."

"Great," I said.

"But before you head up there, let me show you how our water system works."

Kris and I followed him to the back of the hut where a small water barrel sat tucked under a counter. Gator gave us a quick lesson on how to refill it with snow from the glacier.

Staying in the ranger hut felt like a total extravagance to me. But I certainly wasn't going to complain. Kris and I spent the rest of the afternoon and evening watching climbers come and go and enjoying Gator's company. That night we slept soundly, secure in the comfort of a solid shelter.

The next morning, we enjoyed fresh blueberry pancakes, just as I'd promised. Then Gator left Kris and me to our own devices and took off to patrol the mountain. Just like when the boys were young, I had planned an interim day when we could relax and explore, and Kris could soak up the climbing culture.

While Kris checked out every corner of the camping area and chatted with people returning from the summit, I had other ideas.

The hut felt cozy but dark, so I spent some time sitting outside on a rock with my back to the sun-drenched front wall, facing the massive northeast face of Mount Rainier. While I watched climbers work their way up and down the route, I worked on a small cross-stitch project that I had slipped into my pack. The intense sunshine coming from the bright-blue sky made it impossible to look at the white snow and massive glaciers with their crosswise blue slashes when not wearing sunglasses.

I couldn't believe I was lucky enough to spend time here with nothing to do but enjoy the awesome view. With no stress of a summit attempt looming ahead, I felt totally relaxed. Up here, our world consisted of nothing but black rocks, white snow, and blue sky. I basked in the view, though I knew that climbers who spend weeks in this kind of environment develop a thirst for bright colors. That was one reason why manufacturers made tents that were yellow and green, blue and red.

While we enjoyed our day, the Park's sanitation engineer, Roger Drake, showed up. He oversaw the operation and maintenance of all the outhouses and toilets on the trails throughout the Park. During his tenure, he had introduced several innovative ideas to handle human waste. He had also initiated a pilot project in the Park featuring toilets that used the energy of the sun to break down waste. His crew built the first of these "solar toilets" in Summerland, and he kept a close eye on it to see how well it worked.

Roger also built replacements for the little wooden box toilets found adjacent to many of the campsites, like the new one that sat hidden in the trees near the Glacier Basin camp. It was just like the one Kris and I encountered on our first hike to Lake Ann. In the Park, one- or two-sided privacy fences sheltered those boxes that were set up in open areas. More often than not, though, they were tucked into quiet corners, surrounded by trees near the camp.

When Roger approached, we introduced ourselves.

"You're staying in the hut with Gator?" he asked.

"Yes, just for one more night," I said.

"I'm only staying one night, too," he told us. "I've got to shovel out the outhouse, and then I'll head back down tomorrow."

"Really? You have to shovel out the outhouse?" Kris was astonished.

"It's so busy up here that if we don't shovel it out, it'll fill up," Roger said.

"Where do you put it?" Kris asked.

"Have you seen those barrels down there by the outhouse? We shovel it into plastic bags and then put them in a barrel. At the end of the season, we'll helicopter them out."

I was familiar with the old-fashioned wooden outhouse that perched on the edge of the Winthrop Glacier. It provided a great view of the glacier, but avalanches that poured off the Prow during the winter regularly knocked it off its foundation. When Kris and I had passed by it the day before, I'd noticed the black barrels sitting in the snow near the structure.

"We're thinking about putting a solar toilet up here," Roger said. "We just have to figure out where to put it. We'll need to place it somewhere more permanent than on snow. Then we'll see if it can keep up with the waste in this cold environment."

Soon Roger started getting ready for his unpleasant task. He donned a Tyvek suit and found his protective rubber gloves. Before pulling them on, he held out his hand to me, showing me a long, bloody laceration across the meat of his palm.

"Could you help me with this?"

"Ow!" My forehead creased with concern. "That looks painful. What happened?"

"When I came around Mount Ruth, one of those loose boulders in the talus moved on me, and I cut my hand when I reached down to catch myself. I really want to protect it while I'm out there shoveling." He held out a large bandage toward me. "Could you put this on it for me, and then help me get my glove on?"

"Sure." I took the bandage and placed it protectively over the wound. Next, I helped pull his rubber glove over it, taking care not to pull the bandage out of place.

He went out and headed down the glacier. Kris and I looked out the window occasionally to check on his progress.

"That's a job that I wouldn't want." Kris was emphatic.

I agreed wholeheartedly.

After lunch we followed Gator's instructions and replenished his water barrel. Taking a bucket with us, we made our way past the tents that sat on snowy platforms on the Winthrop Glacier. The trail led to a place with white snow that was free of the dust and detritus that blew onto the glacier's surface from the surrounding ridges. Then we filled the bucket and took it back to the reservoir in the hut.

When late afternoon arrived, my mind turned to thoughts of pizza. While I was mixing the dough, Gator arrived and showed me how to get the oven going. Then I assembled the pizza.

I chose a shallow pan that would fit in the space. Spreading the dough up the sides of the pan, I realized this was definitely going to be a thick-crust pizza. The sauce covered the dough generously. Next, I piled on mushrooms, pepperoni, and cheese. Finally, it was tucked safely into the camp oven. We would have to wait to see how this deep-dish pizza turned out.

I left the pizza in the oven a little longer than I would have in my home oven. As time passed, I took a couple of peeks to check on the color of the crust. It was actually turning golden brown! Finally, we couldn't wait any longer. We could see it was piping hot and the cheese looked nicely melted, so we took it out.

I wonder how doughy this crust is going to be? I thought as I took a tentative first bite.

The rest of the crew joined me. The pizza tasted delicious! Surprised and pleased to discover the crust had cooked through, we enjoyed the rare treat. The fact that we ate it in the rangers' hut at an altitude of 9,500 feet made the experience even more heavenly. I felt great satisfaction, knowing that I brought something special up to the camp to share with someone who spent his time keeping people safe—Gator the climbing ranger.

"What climbs do you have planned for the rest of the summer?" Gator asked me after we'd eaten all the pizza.

"I don't have anything going," I said. "Kris wants to climb. His goal was to get to the top before he turned sixteen. But it doesn't look like it's going to happen."

"I really don't want to wait until next year," Kris said.

"I have an idea," Gator said. "In a couple of weeks, we're going to have our Spaghetti Feed. If your mom says it's okay, you could come up and climb with everyone then."

Kris looked at me with pleading eyes. "Could I?"

I considered this for a moment. "I think we can work that out," I said. I trusted Gator. If anyone could keep Kris safe, it was Gator.

"Thank you, Mom! Thank you!"

The Spaghetti Feed was an event that took place annually for several years in the 1990s. It was a couple of days when employees of the Park and a few friends would gather for a potluck supper at Camp Schurman, then make an attempt on the summit the next morning. I was familiar with the event because I had previously taken part in it.

We didn't stay up late, and the next morning quickly arrived. It was our day to depart. Kris and I put off packing our things. We knew we couldn't stay, but we wanted to soak up as much sun and climbing culture as possible before we had to go.

Before gathering up our things, Kris came to me. "Mom, I've got a bad headache. I think I'm getting a migraine."

"Oh, no!" I thought about everything we'd carried in our packs. Sometimes caffeine helped him recover from a bad headache. "The only thing I can think of that we brought along is chocolate. Why don't you try that with a couple of Tylenol?"

He gave it a try, but it didn't seem to put a dent in his pain. It dogged him all the way home.

Still, we left the mountain with another adventure under our belts, great memories, shared experiences, and an invitation for Kris to come back in a few weeks for the Spaghetti Feed climb.

The weekend of the Spaghetti Feed, Kris hiked up to Camp Schurman with several Park employees who were also headed up for the climb. However, the weather thwarted Kris's summit ambitions, keeping the group from going higher than Camp Schurman. Since the opportunity hadn't worked out, Gator invited Kris to come back in early August to climb with him and a fellow climbing ranger, Sean Ryan.

On August 11, one day after Kris's birthday, he was supposed to head up to Camp Schurman. The day was almost upon us when we got a call from Gator. At the time, he was being given more responsibility and was in the running for the job of lead climbing ranger for the Park.

"I have to go over to the Paradise side," he told Kris. "They want me over there for a meeting. I'm sorry, but we'll have to reschedule."

Disappointment filled Kris's voice as he responded to the news.

"Don't worry," Gator assured him. "We'll get you up there."

August 12, a Saturday, was the day Kris would have made his summit attempt. From the lowlands, we could see the mountain rising into a cloudless sky.

On Sunday afternoon we received a call from Gator. "You're going to be hearing about something that happened up here, and I just want to let you know that I'm okay." He declined to offer details, but we soon saw news reports about an accident that had taken place on the mountain involving two rangers.

We learned the details later. Early Saturday, a climber had broken his ankle while descending. He'd landed wrong while jumping across a crevasse at the 13,500-foot level. His party had requested a rescue. In the early hours of August 12, climbing ranger Sean Ryan, twenty-three, and Philip Otis, twenty-two, a Student Conservation Association volunteer ranger stationed in Glacier Basin, responded and headed out into the darkness. Another volunteer rescuer accompanied them, but was soon forced to turn around.

Authorities later determined that Sean and Philip made it to about 13,200 feet where they stopped to fix a crampon. Apparently, the crampons that Philip had borrowed from the gear stash in the hut were giving him trouble.

The summer sun, beating down on the mountain, had turned the upper slopes into an icy, treacherous challenge late in the climbing season. This made having working crampons essential. But something went wrong during Sean and Philip's climb, and the two rangers tumbled hundreds of feet down the Winthrop Glacier. Their bodies were spotted Sunday morning from a helicopter.

The tragic news stunned us. I couldn't help thinking that the twelfth had been the date Kris would have attempted to reach the summit. I hated the thought that Sean and Philip died. I also repeatedly thanked God that Kris hadn't been up there. A week later, a team of three fell in almost the same spot, further emphasizing the danger. Two of the climbers died and the third suffered a serious head injury.

Thank God, Kris wasn't on the mountain that day!

These events drove home the risk that mountain climbing exposed us to.

Because of the accident, Kris's plans to tackle Mount Rainier were postponed for another year. He would turn seventeen the following August.

THE SUMMIT

Keep your eyes fixed on the way to the top,
but don't forget to look at your feet. The last
step depends on the first. Don't think you
have arrived just because you see the peak.
Watch your feet, be certain of your next step,
but don't let this distract you from the *highest* goal. The first step depends on the last.

—René Daumal

Step—breathe in.
Step—ice axe forward.
Step—breathe out.

Over and over again. I gasped for breath. I used the pres-
sure-breathing technique of pursing my lips as I exhaled, to
create higher pressure in my lungs so they could absorb more
oxygen. Usually it helped, but it didn't seem to work today.

My legs burned with the effort as I tried to ascend the lower part of Inter Glacier on Mount Rainier. *If I can only get to the top of this slope,* I thought, *it will ease off a bit.*

I had been on this glacier so many times, I lost count. I'd been involved in at least a dozen summit attempts on this mountain, and additional ones on other glaciated peaks.

I had spent countless hours putting one foot above the other, pushing the weight of my body and my heavy pack full of clothing and gear up a few more inches—*place a foot, push, place a foot, push*—following the footsteps of a previous climber. When I settled into a rhythm involving heavy boots, ice axe, breathing, and pushing, my mind would sometimes disengage and the time would pass easily. But not today.

> *Step—breathe in.*
> *Step—ice axe forward.*
> *Step—breathe out.*

Planting my ice axe in the snow, I stopped and looked at the jagged rocks on the edge of the glacier, trying to judge how much headway I had made since my last glance. *I should have waited longer to look,* I realized. *I still have a long way to go.*

On good days, my progress was discernible. On bad days, like this one, my position never seemed to change.

I pushed back uphill another thirty?—twenty?—ten?—steps before I stopped again, my lungs craving the thin chilled air. I drank in my surroundings while I caught my breath. Two thousand feet upslope, broken rock towers stood guard on either side of the glacier. Between these black rock bastions was the point where climbers funneled toward Steamboat Prow. From there, Kris, Tim, and I would work our way down through the loose, rotten rock to Camp Schurman, a temporary escape from our relentless ascent.

"Mom, are you okay?" I heard Tim say. I glanced up at my tall, slender seventeen-year-old, the "baby" of the family. He looked down the snowy slope from about thirty feet above me. His brown eyes were hidden behind his dark mirrored sunglasses.

"Yeah, I'm fine."

I wiped my brow. Low clouds obscured part of the White River Valley below us, a sign that temperatures would probably remain comfortable this July day. Overhead, sunshine streamed from the clear sky and reflected off the snow from every direction. I felt like we were climbing in a natural tanning parlor. Sweat thoroughly drenched my clothes.

My figure had changed since my first Rainier climb eleven years earlier. I was curvier now, with added muscle, especially in my legs, but I still looked like a young mother and housewife, not an ardent climber. My brown hair was cut short, easier to keep out of my face. My sweaty hair also dried faster when it was short. I even measured an inch taller.

"How long before we take a break?" I called to Kris, who was leading our little team.

Forty feet up the slope, he kept plodding as he answered. "Right up there where the slope gets easier." He gestured uphill with his ice axe. "You can do it."

It didn't seem "right up there" to me. I readjusted my grip on the cool, hard metal of my ice axe, stabbed the snow that had softened in the late morning sun, and took another step.

I should be backpacking right now, I thought. But I knew why I wasn't.

My kids could always get me to do things that no one else could. Now, that included climbing.

It was about the time my high-altitude ambitions faded and my attention turned to hikes through tree-shaded woods and alpine wildflowers that Kris had decided he was ready to climb. He knew then that he wanted to reach the top of Mount Rainier, and he decided he wanted to do it with me.

His dream to climb had never faded since his first back-packing trip at the tender age of six. Details of the dream had changed, though, as he watched me take off summer after summer, tackling glacier-draped peaks all through the Cascades. His vision morphed from just climbing, to climbing Mount Rainier, to accomplishing his goal before he turned sixteen. He nearly made that goal, missing it by only a year.

Thirteen years after that trip to Lake Ann, the calendar read 1999. Kris would turn twenty in August. He'd already conquered the summit twice, but never with me. This was his goal now.

We'd come up short three years ago when circumstances forced me to turn around at 13,000 feet to accompany a sick member of our climbing party back down to base camp. At our turnaround point, I took a picture of Kris sitting in the snow with Jenny Eichler, our friend from Freiburg, Germany. I watched as a tear made a wet track down his cheek below his dark sunglasses. But he accepted the decision without a word of complaint.

Shortly after we turned around, we met another rope team, two men from Alaska. They agreed to take Kris and Jenny to the summit. They made it, but without me. I knew then that neither of us would rest until we stood on that mountaintop together.

Over the next two years, weather and mountain conditions had turned us back at every attempt. Kris had filled out, his six-foot, one-inch figure as strong as if it had been made to haul a heavy pack. While Tim had caught up with him in height and strength, he remained long and lean, his build reminding me of a long-distance runner's.

In the meantime, Tim finally caught mountain fever and joined the quest. He had avoided trails and carrying packs for a few years. At age fifteen, though, he watched as his brother and I planned our next Mount Rainier attempt with Kris's friend.

"Mom, I'd like to go, too." His request had surprised me.

I tossed the idea around for a minute or two. "Kris's Explorer troop is climbing Mount St. Helens in a couple of weeks. If you want to go along, we'll see how you do," I cautiously suggested.

He reached the top ahead of all the other kids.

When it came time for our Rainier attempt that year, Tim and I hiked into Glacier Basin. We spent a night listening to the patter of rain on our tent. Kris and his friend met us in camp the next morning and wanted to go on, but a steady drizzle convinced Tim and me to head back to the trailhead. We packed up our water-soaked gear and lugged our heavy packs to our car. Kris and his friend continued on to Camp Schurman, but hiked out the next day.

Then last year, Tim made it to Camp Schurman for the first time when our little group made another attempt on the summit. We reached 13,500 feet before conditions on the climbing route again forced us to turn around. Even though we didn't summit, experiencing the way we worked together helped calm the nervousness I felt about tackling this dangerous mountain with my sons.

Now we were back again, the three of us climbing as a small tight-knit team.

The responsibility for their lives on this dangerous mountain weighed heavily on me. But having taken them backpacking when they were younger, I realized I couldn't deny them the chance to take the next step, to explore the wonderful, awesome world of high elevations. I had done it. Why shouldn't they?

I thought back to our previous attempt. *My stomach isn't tied up in knots the way it was last year. We may not have summited then, but we worked well together.*

This year my goal was to focus on the climb and push the fears aside. At least that's what I kept telling myself.

Step—breathe in.
Step—ice axe forward.
Step—breathe out.

Focus! I told myself. *Focus on the goal. Remember—you're here because you promised Kris you would climb with him. Remember—you're here because of his dream that you would one day stand on the top together, a dream that you chose to share. Remember—this is your best chance, maybe even your last. The weather is good. You're in decent condition. You're all strong. The mountain is in good climbing shape.*

I reminded myself that the original motivations that sent me huffing and puffing my way up these slopes through thin air didn't come from my kids. I had relished the sunshine, the rugged beauty, and the challenge, and I'd made friends and enjoyed sharing adventures with like-minded people. The harsh beauty of the white glaciers that flowed from the summit, broken up by curving blue crevasses and huge tumbled blocks of ice, had filled me with awe. The flow of the glaciers stood in stark contrast to the surrounding rugged black peaks and ridges. The element of risk added spice to the adventure.

There was a time when thin air had invigorated me as I soaked up the warmth of the sun on my skin. It had made me feel alive to my very core. Back then, my face, arms, and legs were tanned, despite my liberal applications of sunscreen, and I wore that tan as a badge of honor. A whiff of sunscreen still took me back to the contentment of climbing under a deep-blue sky, with my friends at my side.

Things feel different than they used to, I thought. The air no longer energized me. I gasped for every breath. Sweat rolled down my forehead and soaked my shirt. The sun dried out my skin, deepening my wrinkles as I watched. Though I still looked youthful, I was forty-six years old, and getting old sucked.

Almost a half hour after asking Kris about a break, I reached the top of the steepest section of the glacier. The boys were sitting on their packs in the snow ahead of me. Kris's pale-gray shirtsleeves were pushed up to his elbows. He ran his fingers through his thick brown hair.

"We're ready to start again," Kris said as I slowly drew near. He flashed a wicked grin my direction.

"Yeah, well, I just got here." I stomped a flat spot on the snowy slope, thrust my ice axe into the snow, and set my pack down. I pulled out a water bottle and a candy bar, then sat on my pack and took in the view back down the steep grade. Beyond the valley, another ridge rose up. Near the top, to the northeast we could pick out the Sunrise area nestled in an alpine meadow.

"I can't sit here too long," Kris said. "I'll get stiff."

"Just give me a minute."

I chewed a few bites of chocolate and dried fruit, and washed them down with water. Before long, my pounding pulse subsided and the burn in my legs receded to a dull ache. After a very short five minutes, Kris again led the way uphill, followed by Tim. I brought up the rear.

We stopped for water again about two-thirds of the way up the glacier. I looked at my watch. "It shouldn't take this long to get to Camp Schurman," I told the kids.

"When did you think we'd get there?" Tim asked.

"Considering our start time, we should have made it by two o'clock. It's two now, so we won't get there until at least three thirty."

Experience told me how long it should take to get from Glacier Basin to Camp Schurman. We weren't making very good time. When we started up again, Kris set the pace and Tim fell in behind me. A gap widened between Kris and me.

Though I was a head shorter than either of them, I still felt compelled to stay close. Instead of settling into the pace, though, I found that my breath still came in gasps.

"How about I kick steps for a while?" Tim suggested to Kris. Kris happily handed off the lead and the arduous job of kicking steps in unbroken snow. We resumed our ascent and I brought up the rear. Finally, my breathing settled down and I managed to keep pace. I thought I'd found my second wind. Then I overheard Kris talking to Tim.

"Why are you going so slow?"

"I figured this way it would be easier for Mom to keep up," Tim said.

"I can't go at this pace," Kris declared. He liked the other method better and moved into the lead again. Only one thing kept my ego from deflating completely. As we worked our way through the crevasses on the upper part of the glacier, we caught up with a group of three men. A red-faced member of their team, with a generous belly that sagged over his pack's hip belt, stopped about every twenty feet. Every time, he leaned on his ice axe and gasped for air. One by one, the boys and I passed all three.

At least I'm still faster than someone.

Our last stop before the top of the Prow was an old tent site—a flat spot dug into the deep snow. After a short rest, I started up again. Camp was close, and it beckoned.

"We'll catch up with you," Tim said. "We want to enjoy the view for a few minutes." They knew the hardest part of the day had been conquered.

I headed up the last part of the glacier while they chatted like old friends, which they were. I plodded a good distance ahead of them before they started up, yet they still almost caught me before I reached the trail leading down the backside of the Prow. I wondered what that meant for our upcoming summit attempt.

The sight of Camp Schurman below welcomed me at the top of the Prow. I saw a few tents clustered on the Winthrop Glacier near the rock outcrop and the rangers' stone hut.

"Looks like there's plenty of room for our tent," I said to the boys.

"Maybe we can camp over there." Kris pointed to an area in the snow near the gravel spit.

"Sure, let's check it out when we get there," I said.

At the top of the last descent, we stopped to examine the hillside. Kris had experienced this downclimb previously, but Tim had never seen it before.

"There's a lot of loose rock here," I said to Tim as I pointed down the steep slope. "Be really careful. And don't come down directly over the person below you. It's real easy to knock a rock loose."

"Okay," he said. "I'll be careful."

"I'll go first, then you—and Kris, you bring up the rear."

They agreed and I started picking my way down. My movements were slow and cautious, and before long I faced the hillside and used both hands to steady myself. I carefully balanced my heavy pack with each step. Dog-tired by now, I wanted to avoid falling this close to camp. The kids scrabbled down with ease, and I gave thanks when they reached the bottom safely.

We arrived at Camp Schurman around four in the afternoon and quickly located a place for our blue-and-yellow climbing tent. After a short rest, we used our shovel and ice axes to scrape the snow, smoothing out an abandoned tent site on the Winthrop Glacier. Erecting our domed-shaped tent didn't take long. I made sure to bury extra snow stakes deep in the snow to anchor it securely, keeping the winds in mind.

Sand and grit from nearby rocks dusted the surface of the glacier. A pile of dark, rugged volcanic rocks, only a few steps from our front door, provided a great place to spread our sweaty clothes out to dry. Then we fired up our little camp stove and prepared a delicious dinner of freeze-dried food. The menu for the evening included stroganoff and bean casserole out of two foil bags. All we had to do was add water. We counted down the minutes until we could dig in.

Kris searched through the gear in his pack. "I can't find my spoon anywhere," he lamented.

"I'll share mine with you," Tim offered.

When the time came, we took turns dipping our spoons into the bags and scooping out steaming bites of nourishment. By then I knew that anything tastes good after experiencing a day like the one we'd just had.

While we ate, we worked out the final details of our climbing plan. Most people try to sleep during the evening, then start up the mountain sometime after midnight. We had a different idea. We wanted to get to the top in time to watch the sunrise from the summit. Kris had first tossed out this idea a couple of years earlier, but this would be our first attempt to make it a reality.

"So, tonight we're sleeping here all night, right?" Tim asked.

"That's the plan," I said. "It'll give us a chance to rest up after today. Then we'll start late in the day and climb through the night."

"What time do you think we should start?" Kris asked.

"Let's see." I paused to calculate times. "Average time to the top is about eight hours. When's sunrise?"

"About five thirty," Kris answered.

"Sooo, eight hours before that would be nine thirty. But we should add in some extra time in case we're slow."

"Yeah, and at nine thirty, it'll be close to dark," Tim said.

"What do you think of starting at eight o'clock tomorrow evening?" I suggested. They were fine with that. "We should try to get as much sleep tonight as we can."

After dinner we approached the climbing hut to chat with the rangers, Joe, Dee, and Asha. We had met Joe Puryear and

Dee Patterson the year before, when we'd made an unsuccessful attempt to reach the summit. Asha, a volunteer ranger, planned to go to the summit with the other two rangers the next day.

The three of them sat on the stone bench along the side of the hut, enjoying the evening sun. As we approached, they raised their hands and nodded a friendly greeting.

Joe, a brawny figure nearly six feet tall, stood up. "Would you like to see the inside of the hut?" He gave us a welcoming smile. His face was framed by dark, wild hair and a full beard and mustache.

Though Kris and I had visited the hut previously, everything at Camp Schurman was new to Tim. "Sure," he said.

Dee joined us. He wore his hair cut close to his scalp, and his tanned, clean-shaven face was a testament to time spent in the sun. His keen intelligence showed through his dark-brown eyes. Before we went into the hut, he pointed to an area behind it. "See those metal pipes?" he asked. A pile of these, about ten feet long—several of them bent at a nearly forty-five-degree angle—lay in an untidy heap on the rocky ground. "They're waiting to be hauled down the mountain. Sometime during this last winter, they were damaged when a storm triggered an avalanche that came down off the Prow."

"That's impressive." I looked at them in amazement.

I remembered seeing the pipes in years past, sticking up from the roof, supporting radio antennae and weather instruments. Now, they provided a stark reminder of the awesome forces that can be unleashed in this corner of the world. Avalanches came down at regular intervals near the place the old outhouse had stood, but I'd never heard of one coming toward the hut.

How big an avalanche was it, I thought, *to do this kind of damage?*

We entered the hut and Tim got his tour. Afterward, we spread out and sat on the bunks hanging from the walls.

"What do you guys do when you're not up here?" Kris asked.

"We've been going some other places to climb," Joe told him.

"Mountaineering?" Tim asked.

"That, and some rock climbing, too." Dee told us some of the places in the Cascades that he and Joe had explored.

"We've got another trip coming up in a week," Joe added. "We're headed up north to climb Prusik Peak in the Enchantments."

I pictured the steep spire that was so attractive to hardcore rock climbers. "That should be fun," I said.

"We're really looking forward to it," Dee said.

As we continued to chat, the rangers kept looking down the Emmons Glacier, watching for approaching climbers. Most people who were headed to Camp Schurman could take the alternate route up the glacier, thereby avoiding the route we had taken down the loose rock of Steamboat Prow. However, crevasses provided danger for climbers as they navigated the Emmons.

When Joe saw about a dozen climbers strung out across the glacier, making their way slowly up to the camp, he started singing a melody: "Doot-doot-do-di-do-di-doot-doot-dooo-doot." It was the theme song played by the Ringling Brothers Barnum and Bailey Circus Band. The boys and I looked at him with curiosity.

"When we see a group that big," he said with a smirk, "we know it's going to be a circus." We laughed at his explanation.

When we noticed the sun approaching the ridge to the west, we headed for our tent site.

Temperatures began to drop immediately once the sun dipped behind Curtis Ridge, a rotten wall of rock several hundred yards across the Winthrop Glacier. The boys and I decided to crawl into our sleeping bags. Before long I fell into a restless sleep.

About six-thirty the next morning, I woke up and made a trip to the outhouse. Again, clouds filled the valleys below, but bright sunshine bathed the mountaintops and glaciers around us. The snow-covered slopes of Mount Rainier towered above, framed by an intensely blue sky. Even at this early hour, the reflected sunshine hurt my eyes when I looked at the upper mountain. Even so, I couldn't help but spend several minutes squinting at the route, picking out distant teams of climbers slowly ascending the white cone.

The jingle and rattle of climbing equipment caught my attention. I watched as the three rangers stepped out from the rock-covered area in front of their hut and headed up the mountain. They practically trotted as they moved away from the little camp. I headed back to my tent for a little more sleep.

The boys and I had planned to sleep in as long as possible, but—again—tent walls don't give much privacy.

Less than an hour after I'd slipped back into my sleeping bag, the voices of two people talking near our tent roused me again. I tried to muffle their voices by pulling a jacket across my head. I grimaced when I heard them mention they had moved away from their own group of tents further out on the glacier so they wouldn't disturb their climbing mates. After several minutes of trying to doze through their chitchat, I gave up and stuck my head out my tent door. They were standing a short distance away in their boot liners. One wore a pile vest over his polypropylene shirt. The other was wearing a hat with earflaps sticking out to the sides.

"Do you think you could find another place to visit?" I spoke softly, trying not to disturb Kris and Tim.

They looked at me, startled. "Oh, sorry," the one with the hat said. They shuffled off in the direction of the rock spit.

Kris groaned as I snuggled back down in my bag.

"Why'd you have to do that?" he asked.

"Because I couldn't sleep through their talking."

"Well, I was asleep, but thanks to you, I'm not now."

Tim rolled over and tried to ignore us.

So much for sleeping in. Still, another hour passed before all three of us left the warmth of our sleeping bags, dressed, and were ready for breakfast.

As we fixed our morning meal, we kept track of the climbing parties on the mountain, who looked like tiny strings of black dots in a vast expanse of white snow and blue crevasses. We watched the progress of the rangers with amazement as they passed first one and then another rope team on the upper mountain. They moved with a speed and purpose that few could match.

"They're just like the 'German animals,'" Kris said.

Now that the rangers were gone, Tim and I moved up by their hut and took advantage of the stone benches against the walls. We basked in the warmth of reflected morning sun and enjoyed the sweeping views of distant blue mountain ridges. I took my book and binoculars and sat on a rock near the front door.

The view from this vantage point encompassed the mountain all the way from the camp to the top, and I took frequent breaks from my reading to watch the progress of the various climbing groups. Every once in a while, a hummingbird came along and buzzed by my head or Tim's, evidently looking for a source of nectar. We marveled at their persistence.

"What do they find to feed on at this altitude?" Tim asked.

A blur of wings hovered a foot in front of my face, then hummed back down the Emmons Glacier.

"I don't know," I said. "I saw a couple of flowers up on the Prow, but I can't imagine that's enough to supply them with much nectar." A few scattered stems of purple Cusick's speedwell and Jacob's ladder were the only flowers I'd found growing in the loose pumice.

Tim went back to the tent, and Kris came up to the hut to sit with me.

"Mom, what have you done to your book?"

I held up my reading material, part of a thick paperback that had been over five hundred pages long. I'd read over half of the book before the trip, so I'd cut it along the spine and left the first three hundred pages at home. I'd had to overcome pangs of guilt to make the first slice with the razor, but I managed to cut out a half pound of weight.

"How can you ruin a book like that?" he asked.

"It's only a paperback, Kris," I said, trying to convince him—and myself—that it wasn't a crime.

"But what if someone wants to read it when you're done?"

"Then I'll tape it back together or something." I shrugged. "I didn't throw away the other half."

He still looked skeptical. Even Dee found my weight-saving tactic amusing when he saw it later.

The rangers returned from their climb at about ten thirty. It had taken them only four hours!

"How did you make the round trip so fast?" Kris asked.

Dee smiled and nodded toward Joe. "He and another ranger set a record earlier this summer for the fastest time from Camp Schurman to the summit—one hour and fifty-six minutes."

Kris's and Tim's eyes widened. What animals! How could anyone run up and down that mountain so fast?

"It'll probably take us at least seven hours to reach the top," I admitted.

We abandoned our perches by the hut so we wouldn't be in their way as they unpacked and spread their gear out to dry. Tim found a place in the rocks nearby to read, and Kris wandered around, checking out his gear and talking to the rangers.

After a while, Joe offered us some tea, and we followed him into the hut. Inside, we chatted more about the route up the mountain and our plans for the next day.

"Kris and I have been trying to reach the top together for several years," I said. "And Tim joined us last year, but we didn't make it."

"I hope you have better luck this time," Dee said.

"Kris decided he wants to see the sunrise from the top," I told the rangers.

"We'll have to leave in the evening to get there in time," Kris said.

"Are you sure you want to climb at night?" Joe asked. "It's going to be really cold up there."

Dee explained that during the past few days, a steady twenty- to thirty-mile-per-hour wind had been blowing across the top of the mountain. "High temperatures during the day have been hitting about twenty-five degrees on the summit," he said. "The lows are dipping to ten to fifteen degrees at night."

I dug my weather radio out of the pocket where I'd stashed it so I could check the forecast every so often.

Joe, Kris, and I walked to the front of the hut and listened to the scratchy transmission. I held the radio as still as possible, trying to zero in on the best reception. Through the static, we heard someone predicting that the freezing level would drop to 10,500 feet tonight—1,000 feet higher than Camp Schurman.

"I hope you guys have down jackets," Joe said.

We assured him we would be okay.

We didn't have any down clothing, but we planned to carry several layers of fuzzy pile clothes along with our GORE-TEX shells. I worried about Tim's feet. His leather boots hadn't kept his feet dry on Inter Glacier on the way up. But he planned to carry dry socks in his pack so he could change at the summit if necessary. Yes, it would be a cold trip, but we were confident in our preparations.

Soon, we headed back to our tent. The day continued to pass slowly. As the sun rose higher, it beat on the walls of the tent and warmed the interior. Even with the door and mesh window in the rear unzipped, very little breeze disturbed the still air. I tried to take a nap, but the tent turned into a solar oven and drove me out.

The warmth and the yellow color of the rainfly attracted bees, and they gathered between it and the tent body. Their buzzing filled the air with a constant hum.

We watched as various groups returned from climbs or prepared to leave camp and go back to the trailhead. As one large group guided by Alpine Ascents International got ready to head down, they tried everything they could think of to lighten their loads.

"Look at all these bagels! Who didn't eat their bagels?" A guide held up a large plastic bag.

One of the clients looked up from the pack he was loading. "I admit it," he said. "I just couldn't eat any more."

"So, here. Eat one now."

"No, no, I really can't."

"Does anyone want any bagels?" The man held the bag high and looked around the camp at the various climbing teams. He looked at Kris and Tim. "How about you guys?"

"No, thanks, we've got plenty of food," Kris said.

"What about water?" the guide asked. "I've got a whole pot here we don't need."

"Sure, that would be great." Kris collected the pot, and Tim and I pulled out our empty water bottles. We were able to fill them all and still had water left for our cook pot.

As the day crawled by, tension rose in my chest. What I felt didn't seem like fear. It was tension that grew from an awareness of what lay ahead—at least eight hours of grueling, mind-numbing, body-aching, one-step-at-a-time climbing through snow and ice and wind up a steep, crevassed mountain. I wasn't looking forward to it.

I kept trying to summon the enthusiasm I'd cultivated during the winter and spring while preparing myself physically for the climb. I tried to focus on the goal—reaching the top with Kris and Tim. My sons. This helped a little, but the knot in my stomach wouldn't go away.

Finally, Kris's watch showed five o'clock and we had something constructive to do. We fixed dinner and I forced myself to eat, even though my anxious stomach wanted to rebel. Tim and I sorted our gear and checked our packs. Kris finished packing first and passed the rest of the time chatting with the rangers. Finally, we topped off our water bottles.

As eight o'clock approached, Kris prepared the rope and strung it out. Then we put on our harnesses and crampons. I took a deep breath and looked up the mountain. Time to leave camp.

All eyes in camp turned toward us as we tied into the rope. No one ever started a climb at eight in the evening. Climbers always waited until midnight or one, so the snowbridges over the crevasses could firm up. Members of other climbing groups paused in their own activities as they realized what we were doing.

The three rangers stood on the flat stones in front of their hut and wished us luck. At 8:10 p.m., I stepped from the dirt of Camp Schurman and onto the Emmons Glacier, leading our rope team up the snowy slope that rose above the camp. Tim followed in second position and Kris brought up the rear. Snow crunched under our boots as the jingle of carabiners rang through the air.

As the rope stretched out and I walked slowly up the hill, the strains of the circus theme song reached my ears. I looked back at the rangers as Dee waved and they gave us big grins. The sun dipped behind Curtis Ridge, off to our right.

The soft snow under our crampons soon firmed up. We followed a well-packed trail for the first few hundred yards until we reached Emmons Flats. At this fairly level area on the glacier, only a couple hundred feet higher than Camp Schurman, the footprints spread out and cut a wide, uneven swath through the snow.

As we left the Flats and started gaining altitude again, I realized I was in trouble. As much as Kris wanted me to lead, I knew I couldn't do it. I'd always been a good follower, but I usually struggled in the lead position and this time was no different. Trying to figure out the trail and make decisions about which way to go always stressed me out and sapped my energy.

I stopped and called back to Tim.

"Have Kris come up."

"What?"

I breathed deeper. "Have Kris come up!"

I caught my breath as he approached. Then I said, "Kris, I'm really having trouble."

"Do you want me to lead?"

"It's either that, or you can let me stay in camp and you can go up later with another group," I said.

"You're not staying in camp! Mom, you're going up with us!"

With that, I relinquished the lead and settled into the role of bringing up the rear.

A little farther up the slope we skirted a gaping blue-walled crevasse that seemed bottomless.

"Hold up a minute," Tim called.

Kris kept going until the tug of the rope drew him up short. Then he stopped.

Tim dug out his camera and moved closer to the edge of the gaping hole in the snowy glacier.

"What are you doing?" Kris asked.

"I just want a picture." Tim peered down into the blue depths.

"Hurry up!"

I stood and watched, thankful for the brief rest.

Tim put his camera back in his pack, ready to go, signaling an end to my respite.

In the cooling twilight, a light breeze caressed us as we climbed. We made great time up the Corridor. As we moved up the mountain, I settled into a good rhythm. My confidence grew as I realized how much better my body was responding than it had the day before.

By the time we approached the top of the Corridor, where our elevation finally exceeded the height of Little Tahoma to the east, the sun had disappeared behind the bulk of Rainier. The year before, we'd reached the same place as sunrise approached. This year, Tim took a picture of the black pyramid of Little Tahoma, its gray shadow cutting a swath across the bands of ashy mauve clouds that covered the mountains beyond it.

The breeze rose and fell. Tim and I added a few pieces of clothing as the temperature dropped, to ward off the chill.

At the top of the Corridor, we exited and made our way around a couple of crevasses as darkness closed in. We turned on our headlamps and soon reached the bottom of the Bowl. Our world shrank down to the distance our headlamps reached.

After the Corridor, the route up the mountain usually angles to the right. Climbers work their way up over snow waves and traverse around crevasses as they negotiate the top part of the mountain. This year, however, the route jogged left and entered a slightly concave area that continued straight up the mountain for another 1,500 feet or so. The rangers referred to this section of the mountain as the Bowl.

The Bowl was hell.

By the time we reached this part of the mountain, the wind was blowing steadily, throwing loose snow in our faces. The dry, unconsolidated snow in the Bowl filled the air and flowed like sugar under our feet. It buried all previous tracks, so every step had to be established anew. Kris kicked steps into the slope, but by the time Tim reached them, drifted snow had almost obliterated them. In turn, Tim's steps filled in before I reached them.

As the boys kicked steps above me, every so often one of them also kicked loose a large piece of icy crust. These came bouncing down out of the darkness and blowing snow, thumping against me and breaking apart into a shower of snow spray. If the exploding fragment bounced high enough, it stung my face with fine, burning ice crystals.

Breaking trail in this kind of snow took significant effort, and Kris's pace slowed considerably. At least now I had plenty of time to breathe—three breaths for every step. It also meant that Tim and I weren't moving fast enough to stay warm. After fighting the chill for a while, I finally accepted the fact that the wind was with us to stay. We stopped long enough to add more layers of clothing. I even put on my thick gray wool mittens—the warmest ones I owned, which I used only in the coldest conditions.

The Bowl stretched up interminably through the night. My headlamp defined my world as an illuminated short tunnel in front of me. Two bobbing blobs of yellow light moved an uncatchable distance ahead. Occasionally, I remembered the jeweled sky above, shining ice pellets in a black, inky sea. But it took too much effort to look up, and during our infrequent pauses I stayed busy with the task of digging out my water or a piece of hard candy. I knew the route exited the Bowl somewhere to the right, and I kept peering in that direction, but I never found what I was searching for.

Kris wore an altimeter on his wrist. After more than an hour of steady uphill trudging, I asked him to check it and tell me how much farther we needed to go before we could escape the Bowl.

"You don't want to know." He faced the slope again and resumed plodding.

I sucked on candy and choked down a packet of GU—a gooey energy gel—to keep my strength up.

Occasionally Kris stopped and asked, "How are you doing, Mom?"

I searched for confident responses, but answers like, "I'll make it," and "I'm doing better than I was," weren't optimistic enough for him.

When he snapped at me, "Mom, be more positive!" I snapped back, "I'm in labor having two kids all over again! But I'll make it. So, leave me alone!" He didn't ask again after that.

Tim had no trouble keeping up with his brother's pace.

By the time we reached the top of the Bowl, I was wearing all my layers, including my wool hat and my balaclava—a poly-propylene covering for my head and neck with a hole for my eyes. In spite of the unrelenting wind, I finally felt warm.

About five hours or so into the climb, the trail finally angled to the right. We'd reached a point where the route traversed across the mountain to circumvent a huge crevasse. We faced directly into the strengthening wind, the icy blast burning our cheeks. I was acutely aware of the drop-off to our right, a steep slope that fell all the way to the bottom of the mountain. Still, I welcomed the change of pace from the relentless uphill grind we had finally completed. We continued moving, straining to keep our eyes open against the teeth of the wind.

Several minutes later we reached our first major crevasse crossing. We had to negotiate around a big gap that opened to our left. At the same time, we needed to climb up nearly three feet from the low side of the crevasse to the uphill side. Soft, drifted snow draped both sides of the crevasse. As Kris pushed off to clamber up to the high side, a large chunk of snow disappeared beneath his feet—but he made it.

Tim crossed a little farther to the right without much problem. But my legs were shorter, and when my turn came, things didn't go as well. When I made my first attempt, my ice axe sank up to its head in the soft snow above me while the snow platform I stood on slumped down a foot or so. I ended up sitting on the firm downhill side of the crevasse. I stood up on the sunken snow beneath my feet and looked straight at the upper crevasse edge, now at head height. The rope stretched taut across my ice axe and I couldn't pull it out of the snow. I needed to step back and try again, but I couldn't move.

I aimed my headlamp uphill and peered into the darkness, blowing snow streaming across the beam of light.

"Slack!" I called.

Nothing happened. I took a deep breath and tried to yell louder.

"Slack!"

"What?" Tim's voice was muffled by wind and clothing.

"I—need—some—slack!"

Finally, the tightness of the rope eased and I was able to free my ice axe. After backing up onto the firm lower edge of the crevasse, I moved a few feet farther along and scrambled across. I struggled up through the soft snow, eventually reaching the upper edge where I stopped, gasping for air.

"Mom, are you all right?" Tim's voice came out of the darkness.

"Give me a minute," I gasped weakly. I had to repeat myself before he heard me. Once my breathing and heart rate were back under control, I shouted into the darkness above, "Okay, I'm ready."

Ahead lay more crevasses for us to deal with, but the crossings all went smoothly. Near the summit, we reached the bergschrund, one last gaping crevasse. Kris stopped at the edge and gathered in the rope while Tim and I caught up with him.

"What do you think of that?" He pointed to a narrow two-foot-wide snowbridge piled with soft, drifted powder.

"It looks okay to me," Tim said.

"How about you, Mom?" Kris asked in a muffled voice. His balaclava covered his mouth and nose. Only his eyes were visible.

"I guess," I tentatively agreed.

"Okay, I'll lead. Tim, set up a belay and protect me while I cross."

Tim drove his ice axe into the snow, wrapped the rope around it, and said, "It's ready. You can go."

As Kris slowly and carefully made his way across the narrow snowbridge, Tim payed out the line at a rate that would keep the rope taught. Soon we heard, "I'm across!"

Next, Kris set up a belay while Tim crossed, keeping slack out of the rope. Then Tim repeated the process for me.

I took each step with great care, focusing my concentration on the snow directly ahead of me while making sure I didn't catch my crampons on my gaiters and trip. I breathed a sigh of relief once I reached the other side.

At last, we turned up the slope. We continued to take one step after another, up through the hard, crunchy snow and up through the incessant wind. The sky remained clear, but hard pellets of snow constantly battered our faces.

I kept telling myself, *This has got to end. This has got to end.* I knew it couldn't go on forever.

> *Step—breathe in.*
> *Step—ice axe forward.*
> *Step—breathe out.*

I paused and looked up beyond Kris. *Could that really be the summit, at last?* I looked to my right, toward Liberty Cap. *Are we high enough to be almost there?*

I can't breathe, I can't breathe. For the umpteenth time, I pawed ineffectually with my mittened hand at the balaclava covering my nose, trying to push it down under my chin. If I could only get a good breath without freezing. Under my hood, the balaclava kept sliding up over my mouth and nose. I struggled to suck air through the moist fabric.

To make matters worse, Kris had picked up the pace—one and a half steps to every breath. He sensed the summit ahead. I couldn't fix my balaclava unless I stopped, but none of us wanted to stop. The wind never let up, and if we paused, it immediately tried to rob us of our body heat. No, it was easier to keep gasping for air, trying unsuccessfully every so often to clear my face, and to keep pushing up, slowly, one step after another.

> *Step—breathe in.*
> *Step—ice axe forward.*
> *Step—breathe out.*

I looked up one more time. Kris stood unmoving in the darkness, looking back at me. Beyond him, I couldn't see any more mountain. He'd stepped off the snow, and under his feet I saw the ice-encrusted dirt of the summit.

I now faced one of the hardest parts of any climb—when the leader has reached the top, and I still have sixty feet of rope ahead of me before I get to join him. *Turn off the brain, don't look up, just keep putting one foot in front of the other.* Finally! *Finally!* I'm there.

In the dim, predawn light, I joined Kris and Tim at the summit.

"You made it!" I heard Kris's muffled voice. He gathered me in his arms for a bear hug.

"*We* made it," I murmured, and reached toward Tim for another hug.

As I looked around, I realized that in all the previous Rainier climbs I'd made, I had never before arrived at the very highest point of the mountain before unroping. The top of Rainier is a crater that slopes a little. When you climb, you usually call it a success when you reach the crater rim, where you can untie and rest. Then you can follow the rim to the true summit, Columbia Crest. On this climb, we actually topped out at the very highest point. This time, all directions led down.

Kris checked his watch: a quarter to five in the morning. He looked around. "Let's find someplace where we can sit down."

The icy wind blowing across the summit had left a thin coating of rime on the claylike dirt, small rocks, and pebbles of the crater rim. We realized the rangers' warning of temperatures around fifteen degrees had been accurate, the wind making it feel even colder. It was essential that we find shelter if we were going to wait for the sun to come up. Stars still twinkled overhead, and the gray light in the east barely softened the dark sky. Our headlamps illuminated the dark rocks around us. It would be at least a half hour before the sun peeked above the horizon.

Below us, inside the crater rim to our left, we spotted a group of large rocks. I recognized them. These included Register Rock, where the sign-in book in its small metal container was located. I pointed. "We might be able to get out of the wind down there."

With icy gusts at our backs, we headed in that direction, hoping the rocks would provide some shelter.

The surface, frosted with fragile ice, crunched and crumbled as we walked across it. The frozen dirt melted to mud under our feet, adhering to our crampons like cement. Ghostly tendrils of steam rose from the dirt, evidence of volcanic warmth just a few feet below the surface of the rim. Hoarfrost formed long crystals on the downwind sides of larger rocks as the icy wind rushed over them. Down near the register, we took off our packs. We pulled out our Mylar emergency blankets and any clothing we had left in our packs.

I already wore every piece of clothing from my pack except for one thin shirt, and I wasn't about to take anything off just to get that extra shirt on. Fingers of cold wind wended their way through my layers of shirts and jackets. The sweat that I'd been producing from head to toe undermined the efficiency of my climbing clothes.

I looked at Kris. His outer layer consisted of his thick fleece sweater. "Where's your jacket?" He made it all the way to the top without putting on his outer jacket, the one that protected against wind.

He started shivering. "I didn't want to stop and dig it out," he said. "Besides, I was warm enough as long as we kept moving." He dug his extra clothes out of his pack and added them to his layers.

I started arranging the red-and-silver emergency blankets and our packs, trying to build protection from the wind.

Tim stood nearby. "Hey." He pointed past the bulk of the mountain toward a small cluster of lights in the lowlands to the northwest. "Is that Seattle?"

Kris and I looked over. "No," I said. "You can't see it from here because of that part of the mountain sticking out." Liberty Cap loomed in the darkness, its snowcap faintly reflecting starlight. I pointed to the closest area sprinkled with lights. "That group of lights might be Enumclaw. And the one in the distance might be Bellevue, along with the other towns on the east side of Lake Washington."

Tim looked around. Spotting scattered pinpoints of lights and a few clusters off to the east, he pointed again. "What are those?"

"That one is probably Ellensburg." I pointed northeast. Then pointing farther right I said, "And that one might be

Yakima." I paused. "And beyond that is the rest of the United States."

"That'll work," he said. With that, he turned his back to the east and lowered his pants to moon the whole country.

This gesture took me totally by surprise. Adding to my amazement was the fact that he'd bared so much skin to the icy wind. Kris and I laughed while Tim pulled his clothing back into place. Then we resumed our efforts to arrange our shelter.

We sat down together, huddling close to share body heat, Kris on one side of me, and Tim on the other. We pulled the emergency blankets around and over us. The boys both wore leather boots, and their socks carried a load of sweat and moisture from hours of plodding through the snow.

"My feet are really cold," Tim said. "I bet my toes are turning white."

"Mine are cold, too," Kris said. "But probably not that bad."

Even my feet, in plastic climbing boots with their insulated liners, were chilled.

Dawn approached, and the stars overhead disappeared one by one as the sky lightened. Kris turned off his headlamp and we continued to huddle together under an emergency blanket, trying to ward off the cold in the predawn gloom. We had piled our packs at our sides to add extra protection.

From our vantage point, we enjoyed a great view of the white expanse of the summit crater, which looked like a frozen lake encircled by jagged, black rocks. Beyond the rim of the crater to the east, ridge after ridge of dark-purple mountains marched toward the brightening horizon. The lights of Yakima still dusted the inky darkness in a valley below. To the south, behind us, more dark mountains formed an apron around the shadowy bulk of Mount Adams, and nearby, Mount St. Helens. Even farther in the distance, the ghost of Mount Hood appeared.

I felt Kris shuddering against my right shoulder. Soon Tim joined him. Before long, my shivering completed the chorus line.

"We could dig out the sleeping bag that Tim has in his pack," I suggested.

"That'd be hard to deal with in this wind," Tim said.

"And it would get pretty dirty," Kris added.

The idea evaporated without any more discussion.

Sitting there, I pictured the next group arriving at the summit, finding us there. *How will I explain to them why we all have hypothermia? I'll feel stupid asking for help. I'll look like a foolish, thoughtless woman, a mother who thought she could lead a climb and instead put her sons at risk.* I imagined that we would look ridiculous. *I* would look foolish. I couldn't allow myself to go through such humiliation. I refused to turn into a popsicle, along with my kids, on top of Mount Rainier in the middle of summer. I refused to become another example of a careless climber.

Those thoughts were enough to get me moving. I reluctantly eased my stiff body out of the shelter of the emergency blankets, away from the warm comfort provided by my sons' bodies. They moved together, gathering the sheltering material closer.

"Can you dig out the stove?" I asked Tim.

He searched his pack, then handed it to me, along with a pan. One of my bottles still contained water. Tim handed over another nearly full bottle. Kris carried two bottles of lemonade that he had hardly touched.

"They were too cold," he said. "When I tried to drink any, it hurt my stomach and made me colder."

I opened one up and looked in. The bottle contained a slurry of slush.

I unfolded the legs of the little stove and squatted over it where it sat on the dirt near the boys' feet. Then I tackled the job of lighting it. This proved to be a significant challenge. Never before had I tried to light a gas-fired burner in fifteen-degree temperatures, at 14,400 feet in an icy wind.

The boys kept warning me to be careful as I leaned closely over the stove, trying to coax a flame from the burner. Finally, I saw a small yellow flicker, which turned blue with heat only after I'd built pressure in the fuel bottle with extra pumping. As low as the flame burned, it still gave off warmth. The sight filled me with relief. Before long, we were savoring the first sips of warm water, drinking from a common pan.

We huddled near the stove, soaking up its meager warmth, until Tim realized the sun was about to peek above the dark mountains off to the northeast. Over my shoulder, a glowing red coal appeared through the gray and mauve clouds that smudged the northeast horizon. We paused to take in the sight as fingers of light slowly spread across the sky. After all, we'd frozen our rears off to see this sunrise. Its rosy touch soon cast a blush on the snows of Mount Adams and Mount Hood.

Tim said something about the camera, but the cold had robbed us of our motivation to search for it.

"We'll just have to store this moment away in our memories for the future," I said.

The sunrise was similar to dozens I'd witnessed in the early morning hours of other climbs. It was true that I hadn't seen any from a summit before. But cold and exhaustion had driven away any extra excitement I might have felt about this one. Only the satisfaction that Kris had accomplished his goal made this sunrise unique.

I realized we needed to drink some more and picked up a bottle of Kris's lemonade from the ground. Chunks of sticky summit mud stuck to the bottom. I wiped the bottle off as best I could with my mittened hand before setting it in the pan of warming water. Slowly, the slush inside thawed, and then I poured it into the pan with the water. Once it grew warm, we shared the weak lemonade, seasoned lightly with summit dirt. I continued heating liquid and we took turns drinking from the pan until our shivering stopped and our thirst was satisfied.

I warmed my hands over the heat from the stove and looked across at the boys, huddled in all their dry clothes, the red emergency blankets pulled around them. Tim hadn't been able to find his extra socks in his pack, so instead, he'd taken his boots off and warmed his bare toes next to our heat source. They'd absorbed enough warmth to turn from icy white to cold red. Next to them, Kris's feet, now clad in dry socks, stretched toward the weak flame.

I examined their faces—scoured red by the wind and cold, their eyes glazed by fatigue—and pride welled up in my chest. I etched their faces in my mind, treasuring the moment and thinking about everything that had led up to it.

If Kris and I had never gone to Lake Ann for his first back-packing trip, if we hadn't met two climbers and watched them climb to the top of Mount Shuksan, if Kris hadn't later decided he wanted to climb Mount Rainier, and if I hadn't spent hours in physical therapy reading about average people doing extraordinary things, we never would have made it here.

"We've got to be sure and sign the book," I said. I got up and walked stiffly around the boys to the metal box. After unscrewing the fastener, I pushed the cover back, revealing the tattered and worn register book.

Searching through it, we saw that every page was covered with signatures and comments, some of them dating back several years. I realized that I'd signed this same book six years earlier. I'd actually been to the summit about six times before this climb, though never with Kris or Tim. I riffled through the pages until I found my previous comments. Then I found a small white space nearby and squeezed in a new entry.

"Do you want to sign now?" I asked.

"We'll do it, Mom. Don't worry," Kris said. Tim murmured his agreement. They stayed wrapped in their sheltered spots.

I put the book back and returned to the stove.

Ninety minutes after we'd reached the summit, another group approached from across the crater. They'd followed the southeast route that passed through Camp Muir. As we watched, several of them headed to the highest point of the mountain for a group photo. Someone asked if one of us would snap the picture.

Tim slipped his boots back on. "I'll do it." He disappeared around the edge of our rock shelter.

I left the stove and moved over to where Kris huddled in the emergency blankets. I sat between his legs, my back to him, and he put his arms around me for warmth. Then he gave me a hug and murmured softly in my ear, "Mom, we did it."

Yes, we did. In the moment, my fatigue overwhelmed most of my feelings of accomplishment. I thought about the long trip still ahead of us. We couldn't claim success until we'd safely descended the mountain. But from experience I realized that in a day or two, I would look back, and pride and satisfaction would wipe out any memories of exhaustion.

The climbers spent only a few minutes at the summit before they headed back across the crater. Then, as full daylight arrived, the first rope teams from Camp Schurman trudged up the last incline. We watched with amusement as the members of the leading group crested the last slope one by one, each one pausing in surprise as they noticed us. They'd thought they were the first climbers from Camp Schurman to summit. They had either forgotten that we headed up earlier, or they missed our departure the evening before.

The leader approached. "Would you mind taking our picture?" I asked. I'd found the camera.

"Sure," he agreed.

I handed him our little camera. He maneuvered to get a good angle and took the shot of Tim, Kris, and me, sitting on top of Mount Rainier, with Mount Adams behind us on the horizon.

Once that was done, we decided to start back down. No climb was complete until you arrived back in camp.

Within a few minutes we reached the narrow snowbridge that had seemed so scary in the dark. We spotted a wand that marked a better crossing about fifteen feet to the left. No sweat. The rest of the descent went without incident and we completed it much faster than the ascent.

Trudging into camp, we shrugged off our packs and rested a bit. Then we wandered over to the hut to see Dee and Joe.

"Did you make it?" Dee asked.

"Yep. It was hard," I said, "and cold, just like you warned us, but we summited."

"Congratulations! Come on into the hut," Dee urged us. "Rest up a little."

We followed the rangers into the hut.

"Let me make some tea," Joe offered.

"That sounds great," Kris said.

"Do you need anything to eat?" Dee asked. "We've got some granola bars you can have."

"We're fine," I said.

"We didn't eat much during the climb, so we have most of our food left," Tim explained.

"How about water? Could you use some water?"

"That'd be great," Kris answered.

"Yeah," I said. "Then we won't have to go out and melt some."

We gave them a summary of our experience and the route.

"We saw the sunrise from up there," Kris announced proudly.

"I admire people who have a different motivation for doing things," Dee said. "Good for you."

Finally, it began to sink in. The three of us had made it to the top of the mountain, together.

We spent the night at Camp Schurman before making our way back to the world of trees, flowers, streets, and houses.

The journey had started years earlier, and it had concluded with a tough, even brutal, ascent. But through that journey, the boys and I learned about each other. Through pain, determination, and cooperation, we forged bonds that won't ever be broken. We learned about each other's strengths and weaknesses through successful trips and times we were forced to turn back. We'd worked together, drawing on our strengths and compensating for our shortcomings. The journey had culminated in this, the realization of our goal. We had reached the top of Mount Rainier together. Not many mothers can hold something like this in their hearts.

ACKNOWLEDGMENTS

Gratitude goes to my husband, Larry, who made sure the boys were well cared for when I went off on my own adventures. I thank him for ignoring those voices that told him I was crazy, and instead bragging about my exploits to his coworkers.

I also thank my hiking partners, Isabel and Annette, who listened to hours of my stories as we hiked and snowshoed miles of trails. They were the loudest and most persistent voices telling me I should publish a book so the world could hear my tales.

I am grateful for my good friends Judy and Ron Hassell, who helped fan the flames of my passion for the outdoors when I lived in Colorado in the early 1970s. Judy nudged along my interest in wildflowers, which led to several of the more recent jobs I held. My desire to work as a wildland firefighter arose partially in response to Ron's example, and from reading a book that I found on his shelf: *Young Men and Fire* by Norman Maclean.

The staff at Girl Friday Productions has walked me through the process of publishing a book, and I can't thank them enough. Without them, this book would probably never have become a reality.

And last, but not least, I want to mention two of my favorite trail companions—my dogs Maus and Pandy. We've had other dogs, but these two covered many miles with me. Maus went to doggie heaven many years ago, but Pandy still hits the trails with me, looking for deer and jackrabbits and keeping me company as I continue to explore new places.

ABOUT THE AUTHOR

Photo © Isabel Ragland

Judy's enthusiasm for wilderness places was ignited as a child in Montana. It was there she learned about the joys of hiking, geology, archaeology, and wildflowers from her parents.

This spark for adventure began to blaze while attending Colorado State University and working in the mountains near Gunnison in the summer. Exploring hidden places became a passion. Discovering new wildflowers became a delight. Basking in the solitude of green trees and alpine meadows, rugged peaks and fresh, clean air became an imperative.

After three years in Colorado, she relocated to the Seattle area and began to discover the nearby Cascades, with their uniquely lush forests and damp climate. When she saw the alpine meadows and grand vistas of the higher elevations for the first time, she was hooked on exploring this new terrain—first with her husband, Larry, and later with her two sons, but also often on her own.

Over the years, her interests led her to a variety of jobs, including working as a veterinary assistant and selling outdoor gear at an REI (Recreational Equipment, Inc.) store. After earning her bachelor's degree in 2000, she worked surveying streams for salmon habitat, fighting wildland fires, and timber cruising at Fort Lewis, Washington. She also spent a summer doing plant surveys in Mount Rainier National Park—her dream job. Ultimately, she ended up back at REI, where she specialized in answering customers' in-depth questions about gear.

Along the way, she spent as much time in the outdoors as possible. Between 1988 and 2002, she climbed six Cascade volcanoes, most more than once. She hiked the Wonderland Trail around Mount Rainier and backpacked into the high country numerous times every year.

To this day she continues to explore places off the beaten path. Even in retirement she can be found heading to remote corners of the West nearly every week of the year.